THE MEANING OF SAINTS

THE MEANING OF SAINTS

Lawrence S. Cunningham

1817

HARPER & ROW, PUBLISHERS, SAN FRANCISCO

Cambridge, Hagerstown, Philadelphia, New York
London, Mexico City, São Paulo, Sydney

THE MEANING OF SAINTS. Copyright © 1980 by Lawrence S. Cunningham. All rights reserved. Printed in the United States of America. No part of this book may be used or reproduced in any manner whatsoever without written permission except in the case of brief quotations embodied in critical articles and reviews. For information address Harper & Row, Publishers, Inc., 10 East 53rd Street, New York, NY 10022. Published simultaneously in Canada by Fitzhenry & Whiteside Limited, Toronto.

FIRST EDITION

Designed by Jim Mennick

Library of Congress Cataloging in Publication Data

Cunningham, Lawrence.
    THE MEANING OF SAINTS
    Bibliography: p. 175
    Includes index.
    1. Christian saints. I. Title
BX4662.C86   1980   235'.2   80-7754
ISBN 0-06-061649-0

---

80 81 82 83 84 10 9 8 7 6 5 4 3 2 1

Contents

Acknowledgments

SELECTION from "The Dry Salvages" in *Four Quartets* by T. S. Eliot, copyright 1943 by T. S. Eliot; copyright © 1971 by Esme Valerie Eliot. Reprinted by permission of Harcourt Brace Jovanovich, Inc.

I would like to acknowledge and thank the following for their help: David Levenson for many good conversations and the use of his books; Richard Kieckehefer of Northwestern University for sending me bibliographies and other materials; John Carey and John Priest, who have been exceptionally good chairmen at Florida State and provided the time and support for writing; my wife, Cecilia, for expert advice in matters art historical and iconographical; Nancy Myers Blumberg and Dianne Bowen Weinstein for their extremely competent and good-humored secretarial help; John Loudon of Harper and Row, who accepted the book and helped me with it; my many students at Florida State who showed (or feigned) an interest in saints over the years.

This book is dedicated to the memory of my father and to my mother as an inadequate expression of my devotion and love.

Introduction

SAINTS are a significant part of the Catholic experience; indeed, one could argue that the saints somehow describe the Catholic experience at one popular and immediate level. There was a day when priests would not baptize a baby who did not have a saint's name. Parishes and schools were put under the protection of different saints, thus giving rise to those delicious headlines still to be seen in the sports section of urban dailies: "Saint Francis clobbers Little Flower." At a more serious level, the saints have defined various epochs of the history of the Church; we know almost instinctively that the Age of Saint Augustine describes an ecclesial situation far different from that of the Age of Aquinas. Saints provide names for some of our cities (Saint Louis, San Diego, San Francisco, San Antonio, and Los Angeles) and some of our holidays (Valentine's Day). It is considered proper to give a Protestant friend a Saint Christopher's medal to festoon his Winnebago's dashboard. Saints, in short, give color and verve to Catholic Christianity.

There is a somewhat embarrassing side to saints, as every tourist who has visited a Mediterranean country knows. How to explain to an austere Protestant friend the incorruptible bodies encased in glass coffins or the statues of Santa Lucia with eyeballs on a plate held in her hand or the large reliquaries with shriveled arms and tibias? Nor does it help when one starts to read hagiography and discovers saints who fasted at their mother's breast on Wednesdays and Fridays or

who never looked directly at a woman after the age of ten or who
spent the majority of their adult life perched on a pillar. The lives
of the saints also tend to be unremittingly and suffocatingly edifying.
Why is there not just one saint in the history of Christianity who
admitted in a moment of weakness that he found the mayor's wife
attractive or confessed that he hated the food in the monastery
refectory and slipped out for a good plate of pasta at the local trattoria? Why, in short, is hagiography so edifying?

These are all interesting issues, and in the course of this book,
some of them will be touched on. But the basic purpose of this book
is neither to add to the folklore of the saints nor to debunk them. I
take the saints, the writings about them, and the cult devoted to them
seriously as a neglected part of the Catholic tradition. What will
engage us in this study are questions such as the following: Are the
saints to be relegated to the corners of popular religion? Is there a
possibility of understanding the saints in some sophisticated theological way? Is there any possibility that the literary tradition of the "lives
of the saints" continues today in other forms, more accessible to a
new generation of Christians?

I raise such questions not merely as exercises in academic curiosity. A deeper motive is to make a case for a reexamination of a
neglected tradition in the Christian tradition. Such a study may be
a profitable source for a better understanding of both the roots of our
spirituality and a tradition that will shed new light on spirituality for
our own time. It would be facile to argue that "great persons" can
tell us more about a particular subject than can more abstract con-
cepts and/or principles. It is not facile, however, to argue that an idea
or insight might be studied profitably through the agency of its
incarnation in action. Christianity, after all, is rooted not in doctrinal
formulations but in the person of Jesus Christ. Saint Paul preached
not the idea of Christ but "Christ and Him crucified." By analogy,
one could argue (and, indeed, such an argument is one of the motifs
in this book) that a study of the ways people in different epochs of
Christianity best incarnated an understanding of the Gospel existen-
tially would be of use to those who attempt to do that very same thing
in their own places and times.

Every student of Christianity will appreciate the obstacles to such a study. There has been a persistent tendency either to trivialize the saints or to romanticize them in such a way that they seem hazy and unreal. When we describe persons of perspicacious sanctity today, we hasten to report that they are not "plaster of paris" saints. The qualifier betrays how deeply we have been alienated from the tradition of saints. When we speak of the martyrs of early Christianity, it is all too easy to conjure up visions of lions and sighing maidens. It is difficult to link in our consciousness the early martyrs with the many anonymous souls now languishing in the Gulags, prison basements, and "reeducation" camps of the contemporary world.

It is this gap between our received perception of the saints and any true understanding of them that will occupy some attention in this book. In order to understand the tradition of heroic sanctity, it will be necessary to "desanitize" our popular idea of the saints. This will call for a certain critical look at the development of the cult of the saints and their place in the liturgical and paraliturgical tradition of the Church. With some historical perspective, it will then be possible to define the saint properly and inquire into the conditions of heroic sanctity in our own era.

My ultimate concern in this book is the presence of heroic sanctity in our own age, but it is impossible to study that subject without some sense of historical perspective. A look, however brief, at the development of the cult of the saints will help us to see why the saints have not been of central concern to the theologians or to many of the spiritual writers of our time. Historical perspective is also important for understanding the conditions and possibilities of contemporary sanctity. Only creation itself comes *ex nihilo.* Human affairs inevitably build upon or react to the historical conditions of past culture. A Pope John XXIII is almost a moral miracle in Church history: He combined an extremely traditional spiritual life (as his spiritual diary makes manifest) with an almost visionary faith in the moral power of openness and the promise of the future. He, in the words of the Gospel, brought forth things old and new.

It should be noted that I am restricting my present inquiry to those saints who are part of the Western Christian tradition. I am

aware that the Eastern Orthodox tradition has a well-developed hagiographical tradition and a deep theology of the saints. I neglect the
Orthodox hagiographical tradition not out of a spirit of chauvinism
but from a fear of delving into a topic about which I know too little.
Furthermore, there will be no discussion of saints or their place in
the other religious traditions of the world. I am aware of their role
in the Sufi tradition of Islam as well as their place in the Buddhist,
Hindu, and Jewish traditions. Since this work is not strictly a
phenomenological one, I thought such an enlarged study of the saints
would be better left for another time or for those better equipped to
pursue the subject. Those interested in a broader conception of the
categories of the saints in the perspective of world religion could
consult the extremely interesting work of Robert Neville, *Soldier,
Sage, Saint.* There is also a brilliant discussion of saints in the Sufi
tradition in Annemarie Schimmel's wonderful book, *The Mystical
Element in Islam.* For a radical restatement of hagiography, you
might consult the provocative ideas in Mary Daly's *Gyn/Ecology:
The Metaethics of Radical Feminism.*

Some background is necessary to answer the questions I am raising. The first two chapters of this book survey rather rapidly the
development and stabilization of the cult of the saints in the Western
Christian tradition. Chapter 3 sums up and assesses the current
theological reflection on saints and assays an enlarged definition of
the saint. Subsequent chapters suggest that the "new hagiography"
may be found in the literary work of our time as well as in the written
remembrances of those who have been tested in transcendental situations where the ultimate meaning of being a believer is stretched to
the limit.

The idea for this book developed from my personal discovery that
some of the giants of modern literature, many of them at the edge
of belief or, in fact, unbelievers, may have given us more genuine
insight into the meaning of the saintly personality than most of our
traditional hagiographers or spiritual writers. It amazed me, as I
guided my students over the years through the fiction of Dostoevsky,
Böll, Silone, Camus, Greene, and a number of other writers, that the
idea of sanctity—sanctity for an age in which the sense of God has
been, at best, tenuous—has been one of persistent fascination. It also

occurred to me that the literature that has sprung like fresh growth from an unlikely source—the literature of the death camps and the Gulag—has a certain similarity with that of the Desert Fathers. There is a difference, of course; the new deserts are manmade and the new anchorites are driven there unwillingly. But their wrestlings with the demonic are just as fierce, as unbending, and as real as the struggles of Saint Anthony with the devil. The basic story is the same: The good person versus the powers of the demonic. It was this preoccupation with the idea of sanctity in our time that drove me back to the lives of the saints; and that voyage, in turn, has set me to think about the possibilities of those ancient lives for ourselves and our own times.

Today there is a great interest in the relationship of the life of faith and the idea of story. The lives of the saints tell a story, sometimes fictional, almost always embroidered, of people who have grappled with the idea of the Gospel in terms of their own time and their own life. It is a story very unlike that of Church history in that it is much more democratic. There are more women represented; the *Untermenschen* have their moment; there is room for the neurotic, the naive, the unlovely as well as for the forceful and attractive personality. If I may borrow from contemporary Christology: Hagiography is Christianity from below rather than from above. If one can strip away the web of fiction, the patina of moralism, and the apologetic thrust from the lives of the saints, there is the possibility of discovering some persistent themes that still have moment for our time: the mastery of self, the absorption of Christ into life, the recognition of the hiddenness of sanctity, the importance of example, the mystery of God's grace.

Since hagiography is the story of Catholicism told "from below," it has been less susceptible to the restrictions of official scrutiny. That freedom brought with it a certain extravagance that, at times, became excessive (as Johann Huizinga's *The Waning of the Middle Ages* showed many years ago); but it also revealed a side of Christianity often overlooked in the official sources of Church history. The story of women in the Church is a case in point. It is generally recognized that women are treated *in extenso* in hagiography; we have the good memory of outstanding figures like Saint Teresa of Avila and Saint

Catherine of Siena. But beyond them is the little-noticed history of the great abbesses of the Anglo-Saxon Church, the learned mystics of medieval Germany, the highly effective missionaries of the last century—these are all stories of immense significance but without their proper recognition or any sustained reflection in the official understanding of the Church's life.

This book has been written by one who is neither a trained historian nor a professional hagiographer. It has been done by a professor of religion and culture in a state university who finds himself more at home with the fiction of the twentieth century than the *Legenda* of the tenth. It is written, however, by someone who passionately regrets that a large measure of the rich tradition of Catholicism lives now in benign neglect when that tradition still has insights that shed some light on our present condition. It is written by someone who is convinced it is possible to go from the novels of Camus to the lives of the saints and not be in totally different or alien territory. It is written by someone who is convinced that history, even the fragile portions of history retained in the lives of the saints, is not bunk. Finally, it is written by someone who believes that the gap between theology and actual *praxis* in the Western Church is wide but still bridgeable. A friend once remarked to me that she would not trade one short story of Flannery O'Connor for every word that Hans Küng has ever written. That was a conversational exaggeration, but it does point up a truth. Theological understanding is mediated in more ways than through systematic reflection; while we must pay attention to the latter, we should not forget that the other, less-precise, sources are also produced by people who strained to find the "treasure of great price." One of those sources is to be found in the histories of those individuals who have tried to live out the significance of the Gospel.

The late Thomas Merton once remarked that a saint is a sign of God. The saint is a *sacramentum,* a sign mediating grace. The argument of this book is simply that we should watch for such signs and we should be looking not just for the latest saint proclaimed in Rome; we should be looking at the poets, novelists, diarists, prisoners of conscience, resisters, prophets, fools, and other wrestlers with God. They may be the true signs of how well God is speaking to us today.

CHAPTER 1

The Saints: Some Historical Considerations

WHEN Mother Teresa of Calcutta received the Nobel Prize for Peace in 1979, the many tributes in the world press did not hesitate to use the word "saint" to describe her. The word is not inappropriate since the general meaning it conveys is that of transparent goodness, deep holiness, and a broad and encompassing charity. In the popular mind, Mother Teresa represents "real sanctity" as opposed to that rather unreal world of figures that adorn medallions, statues, and pious pictures. In that popular sense, the word "saint" has been applied to any number of modern figures. We have not thought it inappropriate to use the term for persons like Albert Schweitzer, Simone Weil, Dietrich Bonhoeffer, Dom Helder Camara, and a host of others. Their claim to sanctity is quite removed from any formal cult such as that traditionally fostered in the long history of Christianity. Indeed, some of the people we have called saints—Gandhi comes immediately to mind—are distant from the formal tradition of Christianity.

Sainthood in the more restrictive sense of the term has been very closely circumscribed by Catholic Christianity both by the formal means of canonization and the equally rigorous means of the control of cult. Of those persons already mentioned (and their number could be multiplied), there is no cult and there has been no canonization. It will be the major burden of this book to justify the wider and more precise use of the term saint while indicating the characteristics that stand behind such a denomination.

Before I undertake the task of redefining the saint, it will be necessary to discuss the rise of the cult of saints in historic Christianity. Such a survey is necessary both to understand where we have come from and to indicate the limitations of that tradition. Even a cursory look at the historical tradition of saints in the Church indicates the term has taken on a rather narrow meaning, a meaning that does not do full justice to the phenomenon of heroic sanctity itself. Furthermore, such a historical inquiry can help us understand more clearly how we have come to ignore the traditional saints precisely at a time when there is a major preoccupation with exploring the roots of spirituality and a renewed appreciation of the role of story in theology. The tradition of the saints is rooted in story, and the purpose of the stories was a deepened spirituality. That the tradition does not seem to deepen our spiritual life is partially a result of the vagaries of historical circumstance.

The cult of the saints began in Christianity as a direct result of the Roman persecutions of the early Christians. Although the Age of the Martyrs and the Church of the Catacombs have been greatly romanticized by the development of pious "lives of the saints," nineteenth-century novels, and Cecil B. DeMilleish film extravaganzas, it is an indisputable fact that Christians were officially persecuted by the Roman government. These persecutions were, at least until the middle of the third century, intermittent, localized, of varying intensity, and originating from diverse motives. But there were persecutions, and they resulted in the deaths of many Christians (the number is much disputed) in all parts of the Roman Empire. The early Christian communities kept records of these deaths from a relatively early period; and by the second century, there is evidence the Church publicly venerated these martyrs.

These early martyrs seem distant and strange figures to us today. Saint Catherine with her wheel or Lawrence with his gridiron appear to be creations out of the *demimonde* of mythology. The fact that the early Church took them seriously enough to venerate their memory, first by annual commemoration and later by elaborate cult and extravagant cultic architecture, strikes us as a bit outlandish. Part of our problem is that today Christianity is part of the accepted wisdom of the West whereas in the second and third century, Christianity was considered a strange religious movement that threatened the peace and harmony of the Roman commonweal. It was one thing for people to have ideas; it was quite another for them to die—and to die quite cheerfully—for those ideas.

The excitement the martyrs caused may be better understood by reflecting on the powerful forces that a voluntary death can unleash in energizing a dissident movement. The world regularly uttered its disapproval of the *apartheid* culture of South Africa, but nothing galvanized world opinion like the mysterious death of the black activist Steve Biko. The facile abstractions about racial oppression now became a specified person whose face could be put on a poster or whose words could be read.

When martyrs are remembered, they are remembered both because of the past events that caused their deaths and because their remembered deaths in the present pass judgment on both the past and the present. People still surreptiously place flowers on the spot in Prague where Jan Palach burned himself to death as a protest against the Soviet suppression of the "Prague Spring" of 1968. That act, profoundly liturgical in its own right, says that people remember what happened to a Jan Palach. That act of remembering simultaneously passes judgment on those in the present who must, for official or ideological reasons, suppress the past.

This latent power of the witness *(martyr)* has been observed in widely diverse cultural and religious situations. Martyrdom in early Christianity was both a voluntary religious act and the product of a cultural situation. Christianity had a powerful model for voluntary death in the person of its founder; every subsequent act of martyrdom was seen as an act in imitation of the death of Christ. Martyrdom was also a product of cultural pressures exerted by the Romans, who saw the Christians not from the point of view of their religion but as a subversive element in society itself.

The reasons the Romans persecuted the early Christians are varied (as well as hotly disputed). The laws and decrees against

Christians went through many permutations until the fourth century, when Christianity benefited from the Emperor Constantine's Edict of Toleration issued in Milan in A.D. 313. As a generalization, we can say the Romans saw the Christians as political and social subversives. The whole social fabric of Roman society was founded on the notion of *pietas* (flaccidly translated into English as "piety"), which is that admixture of fear and love children were expected to show toward their parents, parents toward the state, and the whole of Roman society toward the gods. When that harmony was a reality, the world was not only at peace, but the blessing of the gods protected and nurtured the empire. There reigned the *pax deorum*—divine peace. Christians subverted this process because they would not demonstrate this civic *pietas* toward the gods of Rome. This unwillingness struck the Romans as blasphemous and atheistic (charges often brought against both the Jews and the Christians) on the face of it. Not to swear by the gods when inducted into the armies or before testifying in court or on public holidays appeared treasonous. Were the Christians willing to make the most perfunctory gestures toward the gods, they would have been left in relative peace. The Romans were extremely tolerant of religious ideas as long as they did not run counter to the harmony of the state or the common good. All Rome demanded was that people not deny the gods of Rome. The Emperor Trajan put the matter succinctly in his famous reply to a letter of Pliny the Younger: "They [the Christians] are not to be sought out; if they are denounced and proven guilty, they are to be punished. There is a reservation: whoever denies he is a Christian and proves it by worshipping our gods, shall be pardoned even though he was under suspicion in the past."[1]

The punishment to which Trajan alluded was, in most cases, death. There are also records of exile, hard labor in the imperial mines *(ad metalla),* and confiscation of personal property. In one of the very few records that have come down to us from the Roman law courts themselves—the *Acta* of Saint Justin—the prefect of the court (in this case, Q. Junius Rusticus) pronounced the following sentence on some recalcitrant Christians: "Let those who will not sacrifice to the gods and yield to the command of the emperor be scourged and led away to be beheaded in accordance with the law."[2]

Christians themselves faced the official hostilities of the Roman Empire with varying attitudes. Certain Christian intellectuals of the second century—called Apologists—addressed themselves to the emperors with an argument that rings somewhat familiar to moderns: Christians are loyal citizens of the empire who wish the empire prosperity and good. They follow an exalted faith and propose a rigorous morality. Their inability to fulfill the demands of Roman civic religion should be overlooked in view of their other contributions to the well-being of the commonweal. It was an argument not unlike that made in our own time by various dissenters or draft resisters.

Other Christians, less tolerant of the Roman Empire (indeed, some identified it with the Anti-Christ), were far more belligerent in their refusal to perform the civic rites demanded by *Romanitas*. They saw their refusal as a positive religious duty and welcomed the consequences of their refusal in the most positive of terms. There are records in the early Christian sources where Christians actually welcomed the prospect of martyrdom. In his *Ecclesiastical History*, Eusebius recounts that the mother of the youthful Origen had to hide his clothes and shut him up in his room to prevent him from confessing his faith before the provincial law courts. This was not an idle gesture of bravado on Origen's part; his father had already been executed for his profession of Christianity. Even earlier, at the beginning of the second century, Ignatius of Antioch wrote ahead to influential persons at Rome, where he was being taken for execution, not to intercede for his life: "Permit me to be the food of beasts, through whom one may reach God. I am the wheat of God and I am to be ground by the teeth of wild animals so that I may become the pure bread of Christ."

The early Christian communities responded with veneration and cult for those who died at the hand of Roman persecutors. They were considered as witnesses *(martyres)* for the faith. In a famous phrase of Tertullian, the martyr's blood was the seed of the Church. By the third century, regular liturgical commemorations were held in Rome to mark the anniversaries of the death of martyrs. These feasts were called the *dies natalis* of the saint because it was believed that on that day the saints were "born again" into the joys of heaven. At first, according to the researches of Josef Andreas Jungmann, it was only prominent members of the Roman church who were so memorialized. Early martyred popes like Callistus, Pontianus, and Fabian had established feast days in Rome before the year 250. After 250 (the year of the first persecution that extended over the entire empire under the Emperor Decius), the list of commemorated martyrs began to include deacons of the Church (Saint Lawrence), virgins like Saint Agnes and Saint Cecilia, and, retroactively, martyrs who had suffered earlier than the Decian persecution of A.D. 250. By the end of the third century, for example, the feast day of the protomartyrs of Rome, the apostles Peter and Paul, was observed on June 29.[3]

In the period of the persecutions (that is, until the early fourth century), there was a universal belief among Christians that those who had died for the faith *(martyres)* and those who gave public witness to the faith and risked death *(confessores)* were the energizing force of Christianity. Commenting on the state of the Church in North Africa in the third century, Professor W. H. C. Frend has written, "In this environment confessors and martyrs were held in the highest honour. Vigils outside their prisons, services in the *areae* in which they were buried, the cult of their anniversaries *(natalicia)*, and powers of forgiveness universally subscribed to them, raised their status beyond that of the clergy. Theirs was a full *militia Christi* whose 'storm troops' *(agonistici)* they formed in the fight against Satan. Their deaths were the seed of the church."[4]

One major component of the interest and veneration shown to the martyrs was, of course, their good example for other Christians who lived in uncertain and precarious times. They were true followers of Christ even to the extent of imitating His sacrificial death. In that sense, the martyrs and confessors* were paradigmatic models for others in a time of persecution. Their example would provide encour-

---

*Confessors were those who openly professed their faith before officials but had not been executed. They were honored for their public act of faith, called the *confessio fidei*.

agement for those who might be called upon to suffer a similar fate. Likewise, they were a reproach to those who denied their faith (the so-called *lapsi*) in time of persecution. Beyond being exemplary models of fortitude and bravery, their exemplary lives testified to the ability of the truly spiritual person to overcome the limitations of pain, suffering, and death for a spiritual ideal. This was an important facet of their witness in an age when spiritual striving was an ideal preached by Christians who had absorbed the *Zeitgeist* of gnosticism and Neoplatonism into their Christian world view. For that reason, as we shall see later in some detail, the martyrs became the prototype of those persons—like the ascetics and the monks—who, after the period of the persecutions, upheld the ideal of martyrdom in a new way by the rigor of their personal lives.

If the early martyrs were seen as paradigms of Christian living, they were also seen as the locus of spiritual power. This is a side of the cult of the saints that tends to bemuse the modern believer and scandalize the nonbeliever. Whatever the modern mind may think, it is clear that for the early Christian, the great attraction of the martyrs rested in their ability, both in life and especially after death, to manifest supernatural power on behalf of the Christian community. The intercession of the martyr or the application of the martyr's relics could cure illness, forestall disaster, shield from antipathetic forces, cause conversion, forgive sins, or avert calamity.

This "showing forth of power" (or, to use the terminology of Mircea Eliade, this capacity for "hierophany") was a commonly accepted part of the ancient world view, both pagan and biblical. The early readers of the New Testament, to cite an obvious example, would find nothing extraordinary in the fact that a woman could be healed of a persistent hemorrhage by the act of touching the garment of Jesus (Luke 8:43–48) nor would they puzzle over the response of Jesus to the effect that "Someone did touch me, for I felt power had gone out from me" (Luke 8:46). Indeed, sculptural panels on early Christian sarcophagi often depicted Jesus performing miracles with a wand in His hand that connected the person of Jesus with the object of the miracle. Thus, in the multiplication of the loaves, a scene often depicted on such panels, Jesus would be shown touching a basket of bread with a wand. The wand signified the transmission of power (compare this to the use of the wand by a magician). This power of Jesus was depicted in the New Testament as residing in the early apostles, as Acts clearly shows. Even the shadow of the Apostle Peter falling on an ill person could transmit power (Acts 5:15). Simon, a rival miracle worker of the time, even tried to buy the secrets of this power, despite the fact that he was also capable of performing prodigies (Acts 8:9).

The martyrs were also capable of performing such prodigies. What is more significant about their thaumaturgic powers was that while early legends and hagiographies relate many stories about the miracle of *martyres* and *confessores* performed during their lifetime, their real power became more manifest after their death. It was at the sanctuaries where their bodies were buried or by the application or veneration of parts of their bodies or objects touched to their bodies (*reliquiae*—relics) that the martyrs and confessors were most potent.

There is a great difference between the modern understanding of the martyr and that of the ancient world. The modern world has not lost its taste for martyrs or its ability to honor them. This is as true in the secular as in the religious world. Anyone who has visited the Tomb of the Unknown Soldier at Arlington National Cemetery can participate in the sensibility that nurtured the cult of the saints in early Christianity. The chaste marble tomb with its honor guard and hushed silences, its stream of visitors and festive celebrations, and its wreaths and speeches all testify to an impulse that is directly analogous to the developing cult of the saints in the early Church.

The difference, of course, between the ceremonies of honor for an Unknown Soldier and an early Christian martyr is that in the former case there is no sense of intercessory power or of thaumaturgic ability. The Unknown Soldier does not "hear prayers"; his place of rest does not exude power. In order to find an analogy with the early cult of the saints, one cannot look to contemporary secular experience; one must look back to the sacred world of Greece and Rome, where at shrines to the gods or the heroes awesome experiences of the Holy were possible. In a certain sense, the difference between such modern pilgrimage sites and those of the ancient world is a fair index of what we mean when we speak of a culture that has undergone a significant degree of secularization.

This belief in the intecessory power of the saints and their relics after death had immense ramifications for the development of early Catholic spirituality, the shape of the Christian liturgy, and the evolution of paraliturgical devotion. Such *cultus* determined a good deal of the early Christian architecture, especially in cities like Rome. Likewise, based on traditions found in the pagan religions, festivals were held at the graves of the *martyres* on their anniversary days. This determined places of cult. Soon it became a commonplace to move a martyr's body (or portion of it) to other places, where new cult worship would begin. This accounts for the number of places, for example, where a saint might be venerated in a single city. This practice of "translation of relics" gradually led to the Roman custom of burying relics under every altar where Mass was celebrated. This custom, in time, enjoyed the force of law. In fact, the technical definition of an altar in the present Roman Catholic Code of Canon Law is a "tomb containing the relics of saints" *(sepulchrum continens reliquas sanctorum)*. Until very recently, when liturgical law has become quite lax, no priest would celebrate Mass without an "altar stone" in which some relics of a saint were buried. Technically, as the above definition of Canon Law demonstrates, the altar stone with its relics was the real altar.

The Christian faithful wanted relics, not just displayed in public houses of worship, but for their own personal devotion and edification. There is evidence from the first half of the fourth century that the bodies of martyrs were being divided up, moved from one place to another, and coming into the possession of private individuals, as opposed to the care of ecclesiastical authority. There are also allusions in early Christian sources to the custom of burying relics of the martyrs with the dead as a sign of their own hope of final resurrection and a place in the heaven of the saints. As pilgrimages became more popular (from the fourth century on), so did the demands for relics. Since relics included objects touched to the places of the martyrs, the distinction between relics and souvenirs became blurred or confused.

It is inevitable, given such a passionate interest in the relics of martyrs, that such interests began to have an influence on the "relic market." While we tend to think of trafficking in relics as an aberration of the medieval period, it is important to note that it was a much earlier problem. We have the testimony of Saint Augustine of Hippo in the early fifth century in his complaints about monks distributing dubious relics to the faithful of North Africa.

The intense interest in the powers of the martyrs and their relics was not simply a by-product of the pressures of persecution or of peasant credulity. After the peace of Constantine in 313, the cult of the martyrs intensified all the more. Indeed, most hagiographers and scholars of this period agree it was during this period that there was an increasing shift away from viewing the saint as a model and toward the idea that the saint was a locus of power and a source of beneficence. By the early part of the fifth century, we see the beginning of a literature that was to concern itself totally with recording the miracles of saints, miracles performed in their lifetime, at their shrines, or through their relics after their deaths. These collections of miracle stories *(libelli miraculorum)* were made both to preserve such stories for posterity and, more commonly, to read them aloud in the churches on the feast days of the saints. This practice has been traced back to no less a personage than Saint Augustine of Hippo, who began to collect the miracle stories recounted in his own area after the translation of the remains of Saint Stephen the Protomartyr from the Holy Land to North Africa in the year 415. Book XXII of Augustine's *De Civitate Dei* has a long list of miracles and prodigies that had occurred around Saint Augustine's diocese in his own time.

This close connection between the miraculous and the cult of the martyred saints did not end with the Constantinian peace of the early fourth century. It was in the same period that the history of Christianity began to show the development of the cult of the *confessores* along the same line as the earlier cult of the *martyres.* The Church at peace not only continued the cultic memory of the martyrs but began to deepen its understanding of the notion of martyrdom to include those who lived lives in which they "martyred" their senses or died in the pursuit of Christian ideals. The ascetics, solitaries, and

monks became the new martyrs who suffered not at the hand of
Roman persecutors but by their own volition. The "quick" martyrdom of execution by a hostile state gave way to the "slow" martyrdom
of the ascetic life.

Saint Athanasius (296–373), the great hero of Catholic orthodoxy
during the Arian controversy, did much to publicize the heroic life
of the desert solitaries and monks with the publication (in 356) of his
Life of Saint Anthony. That book was translated into Latin and was
widely known in the West within a decade after its publication. Saint
Augustine (in Book VIII of the *Confessions*) relates how strong an
impression the life of Saint Anthony made on him when his friend
Ponticianus introduced him to it while he was still living in Milan.
The *Life of Saint Anthony* recounted, in fantastic detail, the fastings,
hardships, silences, and demonic temptations of the great solitary of
the Egyptian desert. Athansius made it clear that such a life was a
worthy alternative to that of the early persecuted martyrs: "There in
his cell Anthony was daily a martyr to conscience in the sufferings
he endured for the faith. He practiced a much more intense asceticism, for he fasted constantly and wore a garment of skin, the inner
lining of which was hair."[5]

Other early fathers saw martyrdom in the lives of those who
served the world with heroic charity, who lived a life of perpetual
chastity, who suffered patiently in this life, or who labored selflessly
for the good of the Church. Within twenty years after the publication of the *Life of Saint Anthony,* the great Saint Jerome, himself an
ascetic and solitary, would begin to publish similar short books on
other "voluntary martyrs": *The Life of St. Paul the Hermit* (376),
The Life of Hilarion (391), and *The Life of Malchus* (386?). The
immense number of extant codices of these books that have come
down to us testifies to their popularity.

It was easy enough to establish the legitimacy of the martyr's cult:
If the person died for the faith under persecution, that was *de facto*
evidence that such a person was in heaven and the martyr's intercessory power was secure. What about the cult of *confessores?* There
was, in this early period, no canonical procedure to establish the cult
of a confessor. How could the Church be sure that the faithful were

not praying at the tomb of a charlatan or an imposter? In the case of the *confessores,* there was no single definitive moment of death, as in the case of the *martyres.* The first criterion utilized seems to have been the extraordinary nature of their ascetical lives testified to either by those who saw such prodigies or by the memory of those who recorded such lives. The other, and more crucial, criterion was the ability of the confessors to perform miracles in their own lifetime and, more importantly, the continued witness of miracles done through their intercession after death.

By the sixth century, the miraculous became *the* criterion for establishing the right of cult for a *confessor.* Professor Agostino Amore writes of this earliest period of "canonization": "A confessor is a saint because he performs miracles (both in his lifetime and after his death) and the more numerous, the more extraordinary, and the more stupefying the miracle the greater the sanctity reputed to the person."[6]

Amore cites abundant patristic evidence to show that from the sixth century on, the miraculous element in the saint's life was the norm for establishing legitimacy of cult: Saint Gregory of Tours, for example, rejected the claim of sanctity for a certain Ilpidius because he only performed one miracle during his entire lifetime: *Non potest haberi inter sanctos pro unius tantum operatione miraculi* (you cannot list among the saints one who performed just a single miracle). The same Gregory of Tours accepts the authentic sanctity of Saint Martin of Tours because he performed miracles every day for the edification of the Church *(quotidie ad corroborandum fidem credentium confirmare dignantur).*

Between the fourth and sixth century, then, there was an evolution and acceptance of a distinct type of saintly person—the confessor—who made a distinct claim on the veneration of the Christian faithful. The life of that person was to be a "mix" of the ascetic and the miraculous, with the latter becoming in time the predominant element. It is in this same period that lives of the confessors begin to be published in a style that would be the norm for all "lives of the saints" until some first attempts at historico-critical study would emerge in the eighteenth century. The most important of these early lives of the saints was the *Life of Saint Martin of Tours (Vita Martini)*, which Sulpicius Severus published in the beginning of the fifth century (circa 403).[7]

The *Vita Martini*, written in an elegant Latin style that even as severe a critic as Edward Gibbon found impressive, proposed the life of Martin as a paradigmatic model for Christians of the time. Martin was, after all, a convert from paganism, an indefatigable missionary, a bishop, a promotor of monastic values, and, above all, a worker of miracles. In fact, the *Vita Martini* is an unrelieved catalog of miracles, prodigies, and healings done both in the lifetime of the saint and after his death. In many ways, this book became the model for all subsequent hagiographies written in the West for more than a millenium after its appearance. It was widely imitated throughout the Middle Ages, when other lives of the saints were written, and even fastidious Latinists of the Renaissance knew of it. Petrarch owned a copy and, later, Cosimo de Medici received a copy from his humanist friend, Salutati. The famous Aldine Press of Venice printed an octavo version of it in 1501. One can still find some "lives of the saints" on the shelves of the various booksellers of our own day that echo the format and pious style of the *Vita Martini*.

From the modern point of view, there is one unhappy consequence of the tendency to certify the sanctity of a confessor by an appeal to the miraculous: The intrinsic value of a confessor's life tended to become obscured or unwittingly denigrated by the rather thick patina of the miraculous. While such an emphasis on the thaumaturgic might well have edified the reader in the past, it has proved to be a positive hindrance to even the most sympathetic reader today. Indeed, this might not be just a modern reaction; a number of the early writers (Sulpicius Severus was one) repeatedly insisted with some defensiveness that the prodigies they recounted were neither mere fables nor lies.

It is instructive to glance at the biography of Saint Ambrose of Milan that Saint Augustine requested from the Milanese deacon Paulinus. The life of Saint Ambrose has an intrinsic interest for anyone interested in the history of Christianity. He was, after all, one of the most important figures of the Western Church. Ambrose had battled the Western Arians; he was one of the founders of Christian hymnody; he was an immensely gifted church administrator; he converted the redoubtable Saint Augustine; he was, finally, a Christian theological writer of some consequence. The *Vita* of Saint Ambrose makes passing references to all these activities; but Paulinus felt an urgent need to turn his attention and his admiration, above all, to Ambrose as a saint in the sense that the term was then understood, that is, Ambrose as a miracle worker. There is, then, in the *Vita* an unrestrained catalog of miracles and prodigies ranging from the infancy of the future saint (when his parents spied honeybees flying in and out of the mouth of the future honey-tongued preacher) to cures, exorcism, prophecies, resuscitations of the dead, and so on. The book spends considerable space, by way of a long parenthesis, on recounting the recovery and translation of the relics of the martyrs Saint Gervase and Saint Protase in Milan, which brought about another round of miracles and prodigies during the reign of Ambrose, under whose sponsorship the recoveries were made.[8]

This emphasis on the miraculous was so complete in the early Middle Ages that the saints, by and large, lost any exemplary value as persons of paradigmatic worth and became instead a *locus* of power. That power was exercised mainly after death and through their relics. Relics were essentially passive objects, but from them could come the power to heal. They were also used for the swearing of oaths, centers around which monasteries were built, a "drawing card" for pilgrims (and, hence, of some economic value), a source of civic pride (as in the cult of Saint Mark in Venice or Saint Nicholas in Bari), and a protection against civil and political evils. Patrick Geary's *Furta Sacra: The Theft of Relics in the Central Middle Ages* is a brilliant demonstration of the social value and role of relics in that period. Geary even argues that from the ninth to the eleventh century in Europe the Eucharist was seen mainly as one relic among many others. Geary notes that the Christocentric piety of the High Middle Ages really slowly develops from a much cloudier position in the earlier medieval Church, where Christ (at least the Christ of the Eucharist) struggled with the powerful remains of other martyrs and miracle workers for the attention of the devout.

That the tendency of the miraculous to overshadow the exemplary in hagiography was not merely a quirk of late Roman history or a sign of the emergence of the coming Dark Ages is proved by the development of hagiography at a much later period. The cause of Saint Francis of Assisi in the High Middle Ages is a case in point. Saint Francis died in 1226. Two years later—almost the speed of light by Roman standards—Francis was formally canonized by Pope Gregory IX in the town of Assisi. At that canonization ceremony, the *Acta* of the saint's life and miracle stories were read out as the custom demanded. Those documents are now lost; but at that same time, Thomas of Celano, himself a Franciscan, was commissioned to write a life of the saint, which he did rather expeditiously. This *Vita Prima* was a conventional and stereotyped biography with some miracle stories, probably drawn from the now lost canonization documents, appended to it.

In 1244, the general of the Franciscan order asked friars who had known the saint to send in their personal reminiscences. Thomas was then requested to take this new material and write a second life of Saint Francis. This *Vita Secunda,* then, was based on some valuable primary material about the saint (these sources are now lost *per se* and the subject of much scholarly controversy) provided by people who had known Francis personally. Book I of the *Vita Secunda* relates early events in his life. Book II contains over one hundred and sixty short, anecdotal chapters (often beginning with the telling phrase "we remember") that reflect the memories of the early companions. These chapters often reflect a partisan view of the rigors of Francis's poverty—views Thomas of Celano quite obviously shared. His emphasis on poverty was implied as judgment on developments in the Franciscan order. What is important about Thomas of Celano's second effort is that it plays down the miraculous element in the life of Francis, though the *Vita* does have the usual uncritical elements of hagiography in it. Nonetheless, it is obvious that Thomas wanted to present the saint as an exemplar, not as a thaumaturge.

This is not a *post eventum* reading of Thomas of Celano's *Vita Secunda.* In fact, the general of the Franciscans, John of Parma, felt the lack of stories about the miracles was such a grave deficiency in the book that he ordered Thomas to rectify this imbalance. John of Parma obviously felt the *Vita Secunda* was not a sufficiently compelling portrait of the saint. In response to this situation, Thomas of Celano wrote the *Tractatus De Miraculis Beati Francisci* between 1250 and 1253. The *Tractatus* is a jejeune and tedious work that is mostly a rehash of the miracle stories recounted in the *Vita Prima*. It adds nothing to our understanding of the saint. Indeed, a persuasive case could be made that such embellishments actually detracted from the uniqueness of Saint Francis. An overemphasis on the miraculous shifts attention to the startlingly original *persona* of Francis by reducing him to the level of being just one more wonder-working saint from the conventional hagiographical mold.[9] It is obvious that the editorial additions were made in order to have the *Vita Secunda* conform to what was expected of a saint's life. The original work just did not fit the genre.

The popular imagination never fully accepted this stereotyped picture of Saint Francis. For Christian and non-Christian alike, Francis still remains a direct and compelling model of a different way of being Christian; the thaumaturgic elements add precious little to the force of that paradigm. There is some justice in the observations of the great Protestant Franciscanist, Paul Sabatier, in this regard:

> When one reaches these heights, he no longer belongs to a sectarian group; he belongs to humanity. . . . Homer, Shakespeare, Dante, Goethe, Rembrandt, and Michelangelo belong to all of us, as do the ruins of Greece and Rome. Or better: they belong to all those who love or understand them the best.
>
> But that which is a truism when one speaks of men of reason or geniuses of the imagination becomes a paradox when one speaks of religious genius. The Church has laid such a claim on them that she owns them by some sort of right. It cannot be that this act of confiscation will last forever. To stop it by an act or negation is hardly necessary. Let them have their chapels and relics, and far from denigrating the saints, let us exalt them in all their true grandeur.[10]

The emphasis on the miraculous element in the lives of the saints, rooted in the evolution of the cult of the martyrs and confessors and developed throughout the subsequent history of the Catholic

Church, is not only sanctioned by that Church today but is demanded of those who would receive public cult in the Church. Saints are openly recognized by the Catholic Church only when evidence of the miraculous is present. In the next chapter, I deal at greater length with the development of the canonization process; but I must note here that miracles imputed to the saint in his lifetime or through the intercession of the saint after death are the condition *sine qua non* of formal canonization. The sole exception to this is the case of martyrs whose deaths can be exactly and historically determined as being true martyrdom. Even in this case, an exception to the general law of the Church can only be made with the express permission of the pope.

The Code of Canon Law has very detailed instructions about the role of miracles in the process of publicly recognizing saints in the Roman Catholic Church. Canon Law clearly states that beyond heroic sanctity and/or martyrdom, miracles done through the intercession of the saint are necessary before one can be canonized. For the beatification process (the stage anterior to formal canonization), there must be evidence of at least two miracles having been done through the intercession of the saint. In the case of miracles for which we have only written records and no other means of verification, there must be at least four instances of miracles. All alleged miracles must be scrutinized by "suitable experts." For a person who is beatified, that is, worthy of public cult but still not formally canonized, there is yet another stage of scrutiny and the demand for more examples of the intecessory power of the candidate. Before canonization takes place, there must be evidence of two more miracles, except in the case of those whose cult is so ancient that there was no beatification process, in which case three miracles are demanded. Only after this exhaustive process might a person be officially enrolled in the public list of saints of the Church.

Canon Law does not neglect factors other than the miraculous in its canonization process. It obviously insists on the moral witness of the saint's life—thus canon 2102 states that any candidate for canonization must have demonstrated in life *heroicitas virtutum* (heroic virtue). Yet the determinative factor for canonization is the miracle. The miracle is *the* sign that the person is truly in heaven and can, as a consequence, act as a powerful intecessor for those on earth.

The implications of such a canonical emphasis are enormous for our understanding of the public recognition of saints. In the case of those persons whose lives are well known either because of their proximity to us in time or because of the historical documentation available to us, there can be a relatively easy judgment made as to whether they were or were not miracle workers in their own lifetime. If they did not perform such prodigies during their life, the only hope we have that they will receive official recognition and liturgical cult would come through their intecessory powers after death. In either case, the miraculous is the *sine qua non* as far as the Church is concerned.

It is difficult to overemphasize the significance of this fact. With the miraculous as the significant criterion for formal canonization— and as a consequence of formal recognition in the Church—the role of the saint becomes *de facto* narrowed. However much the person and activities of the saint may be admired, the real significance of the saint is located in his or her power. It is not accidental that saints are relegated to the "popular" piety of the Church; they have been lessened as persons and become mere conduits for favors, miracles, and interventions. The lumping together of saint and sacramental (medals, statues, pictures, and so forth) in the popular mind is a direct outcome of the reduction of saint to the level of thaumaturge. It should be emphasized that this identification is the result of a long and involved historical process. It does not exhaust the importance of the saint nor does it adequately describe the place of the saint in the Christian tradition.

Christians have, on the practical level, been able to distinguish between the saint as thaumaturge and the saint as paradigmatic model. Figures like Saint Christopher have really become "objects" of intercession for most Christians; figures like Saint Ignatius Loyola are not thought of as miracle workers in any but the most perfunctory sense. While Christian hagiography undoubtedly relates miracles connected with the name of Saint Thomas More, very few people find that such an emphasis exhausts the significance of that most attractive of Christians.

While this distinction between the "miracle worker" and the paradigmatic figure might be evident to most, it is a fact, nonetheless, that the miracle worker has a certain bias in his or her favor in terms of official Church recognition. Some recent examples from modern Church history illustrate the point.

One of the most famous figures in Italian Catholicism in this century was the Capuchin friar and stigmatic, Padre Pio. He was an undoubtedly holy man and was reputed to possess extraordinary spiritual gifts. It was a common belief of the time (he died less than a generation ago) that he could bilocate (be in two places at the same time), "read" the hearts of people who came to him, heal the sick and that he was the recipient of mystical ecstasies. He was widely venerated as a saint in his own lifetime (his following was so great and so persistent that Church authorities kept him from the public for a number of years). Pictures of him adorn private homes, dashboards of taxicabs, and the walls of many a *trattoria* in Italy to this day. On a visit to his mountain monastery above Foggia in 1959, I watched hundreds of people wait hours to see him celebrate Mass, to have their confessions heard, or merely to touch his habit as he passed from one place to another. There is no doubt that the faithful who came to see him considered him a miracle-working saint. To visit his mountain convent was to step back in time to the Middle Ages. In many ways, Padre Pio is the perfect candidate for official canonization: He practiced heroic virtue; he was thought to be a *locus* of sacred power; there was a spontaneous cult veneration of him even before his death. He expressed ideas that were orthodox to the extreme. In that sense, he is a "textbook" candidate for the altars; his life is a carbon copy of many other saints already found in the Roman calendar. His cause for canonization, already introduced, will proceed, I am sure, apace.

By contrast, consider the life and career of John Henry Cardinal Newman (1801–1890), whose cause for canonization has also been introduced. We can reconstruct Newman's life with almost microscopic exactitude. Not only did he leave any number of detailed autobiographical writings; but he was a public person, a compulsive letter writer, diarist, archivist, and collector of his own personal papers. In all of these writings and in the writings about him, there is no hint that Newman possessed any miraculous powers (although he had almost a childlike faith in the power of the miraculous) in his lifetime. Indeed, one suspects Newman, who was a genuinely humble and retiring person, would have been horrified at the notion that he could have been a healer or equipped with other supernatural powers. Yet Newman was one of the truly great spiritual and intellectual Christians of modern times. He was a penetrating theologian; a powerful apologist for the Church; an excellent hymnodist; a man of towering spirituality; and, more important, a singular influence for good in modern Catholicism.

Newman, based simply on the evidences of his undoubted deep spirituality and his massive influence for the good of the Church, cannot be venerated *formally* as a saint in the Catholic Church because he is not a martyr (except in the ironical sense that he was the subject of repeated humiliations from his ecclesiastical superiors, an obtuse Roman curia, and a petty hierarchy in Ireland) and the requisite number of miracles have not been "performed" through his intercession after death as yet.

The point to be urged here is that the contrasting lives of these two persons points to an imbalance in the notion of what we mean by a saint. Padre Pio, on the face of it, would (and does) qualify for "sainthood" when one uses the historical criterion that has developed in the formal discipline of the Church. Yet if one were to adopt another set of criteria (something I propose later in this book) and simply ignore the historically conditioned biases of Church tradition, Newman would have an equal if not greater claim to the altars precisely because he not only evinced a genuinely profound sense of what it meant to be a Christian in a given historical period but, and this is far more important, he provided a model for others to follow.

The dramatic difference between the life of Padre Pio and Cardinal Newman also illustrates their divergent roles as models for other Christians. Apart from the communality of their more obvious virtues—a deep faith, a devotion to prayer, and an unbounding charity —the striking difference between the two can be found in the degree to which Newman developed his ordinary gifts while Padre Pio became the recipient of extraordinary ones. In the life of Newman, one can see certain traits that are possible to emulate. That his name is attached to Catholic centers on university campuses is not accidental. He is a model for anyone who wishes to combine spirituality, scholarship, and dedication to the values of the Christian intellectual tradition. The life of Padre Pio, on the other hand, provides no distinctive set of values to emulate. One may aspire to be a Christian humanist and to restate the Gospel in modern discourse. It is an ambitious aspiration but not an outlandish one. But, could one, without being charged with egomania or self-delusion, aspire to be a stigmatic or to have the powers of bilocation? This is not to denigrate the witness of Padre Pio. It is not to argue that the extraordinary has no place in authentic religion. In a secularized age, Padre Pio may well be a "sign of contradiction," but he is not *the* model of "canonizable" saints. He represents the extraordinary, but he hardly exhausts the meaning of heroic sanctity.

If we are to challenge the primacy of the miraculous in defining the saint, we need to do more than merely note that the miraculous is the basic criterion. We need to ask why the miraculous came to such prominence in the early development of the cult of saints in order to assess its claim for continued primacy.

It seems that in the formative period of the growth of the Christian *cultus* of the saints, both martyrs and confessors (a period that corresponded roughly with the late empire and its subsequent fall), the early Church adopted (or better, absorbed) an attitude that was common, indeed, basic, in the ancient world: sacred power could be manifested through the presence of a person or an object. This belief was given in the ancient, presecularized world in which Christianity was born and developed. In that sense, Christianity accepted the pagan idea that religious power can "break through" into the world. One must be careful not to be so completely reductionistic as to say Christianity was paganism under a new name; but it is clear that, whatever secularizing tendencies existed in biblical Christianity, the new religion of Jesus did not make a clean break with the world view it inherited. The Christian saints are not mere replacements for the pagan deities. The saints were, after all, human beings; and they were seen, at least partially, as models: "fingers who pointed the way." The gods and heroes did not primarily serve paradigmatic functions; they filled power needs. In the age of the *confessores*, however, there was a gradual shifting toward thinking of the saints mainly as miracle workers. That shift eventually led to the primacy of the miraculous not only in the retelling of the life of the saint but also in the recognition of that life as worthy of official cult in the Church.

Since it is so often said that the cult of the saints was merely a wholesale "baptism" of the pagan cults of Rome, it is worthwhile to note that postexilic Judaism venerated the memory of its martyrs, such as the Maccabees and the prophet Isaiah. We know of the existence of shrines and sanctuaries in Judaism where heroes, martyrs, and prophets were venerated and prayed to. Christians did not hesitate to accept these Jewish saints into their own cult as time passed. Until the revision of the Roman calendar in 1960, for example, the Old Testament Maccabee brothers were venerated as martyrs in the Roman Catholic Church with a feast day on August 1. Their relics were at one time thought to be preserved in the Roman Church of San Pietro in Vincoli. The Eastern Church's veneration of the "Seven Holy Brothers" is probably based on an absorption of the Maccabees' story. In order to be balanced, one must also recognize the strong Jewish roots of the early *cultus* of the saints.

As the miraculous became more central to the life of the devout churchgoer of early Christianity, it became easier to regard the power of the saints as a sign of the overthrow of the ancient power of the pagan deities. If Judaism provided the matrix for the cult of the martyrs, it was the world of paganism that provided the reasons for its rapid development. It was the policy of the Church authorities to juxtapose the power of Christianity with the impotence of the old gods and their shrines. Gerardus van der Leeuw cites a letter of Saint Gregory the Great to the Abbot Mellitus to the effect that he encouraged the building of saints' shrines on the sites of former pagan temples and sanctuaries as a way to get the populace to accept the superiority of the claims of Christianity. This practice was a kind of missionary accommodation, as the saint makes clear: "He who seeks to ascend to the highest point climbs not by leaps, but by steps or strides."[11]

This sense of "competition" between the powers of Christianity and the older powers of paganism was a significant part of the early cult of the martyrs. The first clear case of a saint's body being "translated," for instance, is that of Saint Babylas, who, while bishop of Antioch, suffered martyrdom in the Decian persecution of 250. About one hundred years later, his body was moved from Antioch to a suburb of Daphne by Gallus Caesar in order to silence the power of an oracle of Apollo that was functioning there. Interestingly enough, Julian the Apostate, ten years later, moved the body of Saint Babylas away from that area with the hope of reviving the ancient oracle's powers at Daphne. The peregrinations of the saint were not over. Twenty years after Julian's translation, Bishop Meletius brought the body back to Antioch and had a basilica built for it. In all of these *translations,* the element of power—the power of the oracle or the saint—was a significant factor.

At least in the sense of the saints as power agents, they became the natural successors of the old Roman *lares* or genius. Saints not only worked miracles, but like the pagan divinities, their intercession was invoked in specific sacred places. They also, like the pagan gods, were assigned specific tasks or responsibilities. This assignment of saints to specific areas of concern was to persist down to our own time. Martin Luther gives a vivid account of such practices in his own day in a passage of the *Greater Catechism:* "If someone has a toothache, he fasts and prays to St. Apollonia; if he fears danger from fire he makes St. Lawrence his helper in distress; if he is afraid of plague he makes his vows to St. Sebastian or St. Ottila; Rochus is invoked for eye disease, Blaise for sore throats, while St. Anthony of Padua returns lost objects."[12]

If anyone objects that Luther is a poisoned witness because of the Reformation antipathy to the intercession of the saints, there are the contemporary strictures of his Catholic adversary, Erasmus of Rotterdam, who notes in *The Praise of Folly:*

> Closely related are those who have reached the foolish but comforting belief that if they gaze on a picture of Polyphemous-Christopher they will not die that day; or that whoever speaks the right words to an image of Barbara will return unharmed from battle or that a novena to Erasmus, with proper prayers and candles, will shortly make one rich. In St. George they have turned up another Hercules or Hippolytus. They all but adore his house which is piously studded and ornamented, and they ingratiate themselves with small gifts. To swear by St. George's brass helmet is an

oath for a king. . . . The same thing on a large scale occurs when sections of the country set up regional saints, and assign peculiar status to each one. One gives relief from toothache, another aids women in labor, a third recovers stolen goods, a fourth succors the shipwrecked, and still another watches over sheep—the list is too long to finish.[13]

This superstitious misunderstanding of the role of saints in his own day did not mean that Erasmus found no place for the veneration of saints. In fact, Erasmus saw the value of the saints to be in their role as models. In the *Handbook of the Militant Christian (Enchiridion Militis Christiani)*, Erasmus chronicles the misuse of the saints in a manner similar to that passage quoted above and then adds, "Perhaps you are wont to venerate the relics of the saints, yet at the same time you condemn their greatest legacy, the example of their lives. No veneration of Mary is greater than an imitation of her humility. No devotion to the saints is more acceptable to God than the imitation of their virtues. . . . Do you want to honor St. Francis? Then give away your wealth to the poor, restrain your evil impulses, and see in everyone you meet the image of Chirst."[14]

What Luther, Erasmus, and a host of other writers complained of—and legitimately, one would have to say—was the degeneration of the saints into demigods in the popular religious imagination. It would be otiose to document this as a fact; but it is clear that such a degeneration set in very early, continued right through the Middle Ages, and can still be seen as a fact in certain areas of the Christian world right down to the present time. This degenerative process was the result of certain religious ideas being allowed to flourish in the realm of the popular imagination unchecked by any theological or peculiarly spiritual refinement. "The medieval church," wrote J. Huizinga, "was rather heedless of the danger of the deterioration of the faith caused by the popular imagination roaming unchecked in the sphere of hagiology."[15] The end result of such unchecked sentiment and imagination produced its fair share of grotesqueries in the life of the Middle Ages: pious crowds pulling away the linen and then the hair, fingernails, and nipples of Queen Elizabeth of Hungary when her body lay in state in 1231 or King Charles VI of France in 1392 distributing the ribs of his sainted ancestor (Louis the Pious) as gifts to friends who attended a royal banquet.

The worst of these excesses were checked by the reforming spirit of the post-Reformation reforms of the Council of Trent, but the reforms of that period had no intention of doing away with or deemphasizing the thaumaturgic element in the veneration of the saints. The Profession of Faith of the Council of Trent clearly affirmed that the saints were to be invoked and venerated and their relics were also to be venerated *(eorum reliquias esse venerandas)*. That tradition, notwithstanding *aggiornamento*, is still part of the Catholic *Zeitgeist*. A quick perusal of the popular Catholic newspapers catering for mass consumption will still feature ads for novenas in honor of Saint Anthony or Saint Jude (the "patron of lost causes"); Saint Christopher medallions continue to festoon dashboards; dissecated arms, fingers, and other parts of the human anatomy can still be seen and venerated in churches all over the Catholic world. As I write these words, the figure of Saint Francis smiles at me from a small reproduction tacked on the bookcase opposite. Old traditions die hard, and rightly so.

It is important for anyone interested in the whole area of sanctity in the modern world to recover a sense of the embodiment of the holy in the life of a concrete person. That means, in essence, that the history of the saint is still an important area for research, reflection, and learning. That is a formidable task for anyone who has turned with eagerness to a study of hagiography to be "plunged at once into the nightmare of early medieval diplomatic and forgery, into all the tangled chronological difficulties of the *fasti* of half the sees of Europe, into the labyrinthine ways of martyrologies, necrologies, and calendars, into the linguistic, social, and psychological variety of Christian sentiments . . . add to all this the theological background and the judgment of credibility, possibility, and moral and spiritual sanity inseparable from the subject matter itself."[16]

That intimidating area known as hagiography is not the only obstacle. There is also the natural skepticism of the modern mind that recoils from the prodigious, the supernatural, and the miraculous. It is not my intention to deny the possibility of the miraculous. It is important to know, however, that the miraculous is only one facet of hagiography. It is a part of the lives of the saints that has a historical origin and a long-standing official sanction. It has been the purpose of this brief historical excursus to put that element into some kind of perspective.

There is another element that makes the saints somewhat alien to our experience. They have been enshrined in plaster of paris. We tend to think of saints in terms of traditional hagiography. We see them, as it were, through a haze of incense smoke. To appreciate better what a saint is, it is not sufficient to understand them apart from the thaumaturgic element. We must also understand that their position in the Church is the result of the particular care the institutional church has taken to make them "their own." In the history of sainthood in Catholic Christianity, the saints have been bureaucratized. Like all products of bureaucracy, they have become somewhat sanitized as a result. They look, sound, and act rather like the bureaucracy that produces them. The process of bureaucratizing the calendar of the saints is called canonization; it is a process that has historical justification and lamentable limitations. It will be the burden of the subsequent chapter to discuss that topic.

NOTES

1. The famous exchange of letters between Pliny and the Emperor Trajan about the Christians in Bithynia (circa A.D. 111) is widely available; it is found in the original Latin in Conradus Kirch, *Enchiridion Fontium Historiae Ecclesiasticae Antiquae* (Rome: Herder, 1950), no. 38–31. The literature on the Roman persecutions is vast. I have consulted W. H. C. Frend, *Martyrdom and Persecution in the Early Church* (Garden City: Doubleday Anchor, 1967) to great advantage; it is especially valuable for its fine notes and vast bibliography. Frend's book is especially good in its emphasis on the Jewish roots of the cult of martyrs; on that point, compare Peter Brown's assessment in *Religion and Society in the Age of Augustine* (New York: Harper and Row, 1972), p. 81. On the complex legal questions concerning the persecutions, compare the studies of G. E. M. de St. Croix and A. N. Sherwin-White in M. I. Finley, ed. *Studies in Ancient Society* (London: Routledge and Kegan Paul, 1974), pp. 210–262.

2. Quoted in Johannes Quasten, *Patrology*, vol. 1 (Westminster: Newman Press, 1950), p. 178. Compare Kirch, *Enchiridion*, no. 71, for other examples.

3. Josef A. Jungmann, *The Early Liturgy* (Notre Dame: Notre Dame University Press, 1959), p. 176.

4. Frend, *Martyrdom*, p. 268.

5. Saint Athanasius, *The Life of Saint Anthony*, trans. Emily Keenan, S.C.N. In

Fathers of the Church, vol. 15 (Washington: Catholic University Press, 1952), p. 178.

6. Agostino Amore, "Culto e cannonizzazione dei santi nell 'antichita' cristiana," *Antonianum* (January–March 1977), p. 58. Compare the same author's "La canonizzazione vescovile," *Antonianum* (April–September 1977), pp. 231–66, which describes the evolution of the canonization process in the early medieval period. These articles, by an eminent Roman hagiographer, are an invaluable study of the early development of the cult of the saints.

7. It is available in English: Sulpicius Severus, *The Life of Saint Martin,* trans. Bernard Peebles. In *Fathers of the Church, vol. 7* (Washington: Catholic University Press, 1949), p. 79. Along with the *Life,* Peebles also translated the *Dialogues* and *Letters* of Sulpicius about the saint's life.

8. Paulinus, "Life of Ambrose," trans. John Lacey. In *Fathers of the Church, vol. 15,* pp. 33–68.

9. All these Franciscan documents are readily available in Marion Habig, OFM, ed., *Saint Francis of Assisi: Omnibus of Sources* (Chicago: Franciscan Herald Press, 1973). I have briefly discussed the tangled problem of these early lives in Lawrence S. Cunningham, *Saint Francis of Assisi* (Boston: Twayne, 1976), especially chap. 3.

10. From the introduction to his famous *Saint François D'Assise* (1893) I have translated and published the entire introduction in Lawrence S. Cunningham, *Brother Francis: An Anthology of Writings By and About Saint Francis* (New York: Harper and Row, 1972), pp. 22–31.

11. Gerardus van der Leeuw, *Religion in Essence and Manifestation,* vol. 1 (New York: Harper and Row, 1960), p. 158.

12. Cited in ibid.

13. In John Dolan, ed. and trans., *The Essential Erasmus* (New York: Mentor Omega Book, 1964), p. 129.

14. Ibid., p. 66.

15. John Huizinga, *The Waning of the Middle Ages* (Garden City: Doubleday Anchor, 1954), p. 166. The same point has been made, of course, by less-sympathetic writers from Edward Gibbon in the *Decline and Fall of the Roman Empire* to Jacob Burckhardt in *The Civilization of the Renaissance in Italy.*

16. David Knowles, *Great Historical Enterprises: Problems in Monastic History* (New York: Nelson, 1962), p. 9. This book is a very useful survey of the development of historical research into hagiography with illuminating chapters on both the Bollandists and the Maurists.

CHAPTER 2

The Bureaucratization
of Sanctity

In order to get some sense of the psychic distance that lies between the current attitude toward saints and that of the ancient Church, let us consider two historical incidents of the not too distant past.

On August 9, 1943 (two years to the day before the first atomic bomb attack in world history), an Austrian peasant was beheaded in a Gestapo prison in Berlin. Franz Jägerstatter was a farmer and rural church sexton from a small village near Salzburg. He was the father of three children, a man of little education and minor means. He was a deeply pious Catholic and, as a result of his own understanding of the faith, a convinced pacifist. He refused to serve in the armed forces of Nazi Germany. His biographer, Gordon Zahn (in his book, *In Solitary Witness*), has shown that he received absolutely no aid or comfort in his decision. The general consensus of his village was that his death was a tragic human waste brought on by an obdurate act of religious fanaticism. Even his own bishop beseeched him to serve in the army, as was expected of a faithful Catholic. He refused and died for that refusal. He was, in the complete sense of that term, a religious martyr.

Had Franz Jägerstatter lived in the early Church and had he died in his refusal to swear the Roman *sacramentum* before the gods, a cult would have quickly and inevitably sprung up about his grave site.

Had his story been discovered, say, in the tenth century, he would probably have been proclaimed a martyr by his local bishop, his relics would have been transferred to a suitable chapel, and the cult would have been legitimized by the authority of the bishop. Had the story been learned of after the thirteenth century, there would have been a papal canonization.

Franz Jägerstatter died in 1943; he did not die under the ax of a Roman headsman. After his death, there was no proclamation from the local bishop and no cult sprang up. Indeed, his bishop, when he learned of the full horrors of the Nazi atrocities after the war, was still reluctant to talk about his martyred parishioners for fear it would scandalize the many Catholics who had "done their duty" by serving in the military. His bones now rest in the parish burying ground next to the village church. People, usually pacifists, visit the tomb. To my knowledge, his cause for canonization has not been introduced.

Franz Jägerstatter was one of the hidden saints of our day. His case does raise some very interesting questions: Why has he not been raised to the altars as a Catholic martyr of the Nazis? Why have clerical figures of the same period already been entered into the canonization process? Without the slightest denigration of the heroism of his life, why Maximilian Kolbe (a Polish Franciscan who volunteered his life for that of another inmate at Auschwitz) and not Franz Jägerstatter? Because he was a layman and had no religious order to sponsor his cause? Because he was a pacifist? More important, why was there no spontaneous acclamation of his act immediately after it happened? The Church, it is said, tolerates war but canonizes peace. That was surely not the case in this instance. By 1943, few people were ignorant about the atrocities of the Nazis. What a figure to extol to the entire world as a hero of the faith and a martyr for Christ! But neither his bishop nor his pope (assuming the pope even knew of his death) spoke. The moral and spiritual witness of Franz Jägerstatter was hidden in his own time; it was left to a later generation to learn about him and from him.

Precisely one year to the day before the death of Franz Jägerstatter (Is August 9 a portentious date? Maybe it could serve as a Christian day of mourning and commemoration, given the anniversaries it commemorates.), a Carmelite nun, Sister Benedicta of the Cross, was sent to the gas chamber at Auschwitz. Edith Stein (her secular name) was a German Jewess who converted to Christianity as a young adult. A brilliant philosopher (she was Edmund Husserl's assistant at Freiburg and, later, a philosopher of note in her own right) who became a Catholic through her study of Saint Teresa of Avila, she taught in various schools until she entered a German Carmelite convent at Cologne in 1933. Because of the racial laws of Germany, her superiors transferred her to the Dutch Carmel of Echt in 1938. In 1942, she and another nun were arrested by the S.S. Shortly thereafter, she perished in the concentration camps. When Pope John Paul II visited Auschwitz during his Polish visit of 1979, he mentioned this brave woman by name.

Members of the Edith Stein Guild (a voluntary group dedicated to Jewish-Catholic relations) have long hoped the cause of Edith Stein would be forwarded to Rome. According to one of its members (see the *New York Times,* August 9, 1979), the cause is a difficult one because no miracles have been attributed to her. Clearly, Edith Stein was a martyr and on that basis alone she deserves the full commitment of the Church. It was not until 1979 that her name was publicly invoked by the highest Church authority as a witness *usque ad mortem* for the faith.

In the case of Franz Jägerstatter and of Edith Stein, there are "problems." Jägerstatter was a pacifist; Stein was a Jew. In fact, their canonization would be to emphasize, in subtle and oblique ways to be sure, certain areas of ethical behavior the ever patient Vatican might not want to overemphasize. Does the Church really want to "canonize" radical pacifism? Did Edith Stein die "for Christ" or because she was a Jewess? Would her canonization somehow bring the millions of dead Jews closer to the consciousness of the Church, a closeness that is still something extremely discomfiting?

These questions are not raised to heap coals on the head of an excessively diplomatic Vatican. They are raised to underscore how easily the process of canonization can be used as a domesticating device to rein in potentially explosive religious issues. The tendency to domesticize religious sentiment is deeply rooted in the historical development of canonization procedures. A study of who does not get canonized is often a clearer indication of the state of the Church than any scrutiny of those who are canonized. In order to understand the good (and the evil) the formal canonization procedures have caused, it is necessary to trace, in broad outlines, how canonizations as a juridical process came about.

We have already seen that in the first three centuries of the Church's history, the *martyres* were venerated by the faithful and their intercession was sought for a variety of needs and desires. Their death anniversaires *(natalicia* or *dies natalis)* were observed and their intercession was sought. They were, in short, the objects of much intense Christian devotion. Epigraphers have recovered from the walls of ancient shrines, cemeteries, and churches the poignant graffiti of ancient pilgrims who came to pray at the tombs or shrines of the ancient martyrs in Rome. "Saint Sixtus, keep Aurelius in your prayers!" "Peter and Paul, pray for Victor!" "Sophronia, thou shall live forever in God!" "Marcellinus and Peter, pray for Gallo, a Christian!" "Hippolytus, keep in mind Peter, a sinner!"[1]

With the Constantinian peace (after A.D. 313), hordes of pilgrims came to pray at the tombs of the Apostles and martyrs in Rome and elsewhere. There was no problem in this early period where to go or to whom one should address one's prayers of intercession. The number of martyrs given public *cultus* was a limited one in the early Church. Their burial places were well known and protected by the Church; indeed, some of the cemeteries were legal Church property even before the persecutions were ended. Their *cultus* was regulated by the liturgical law of the Church. In this early period, the equivalent of canonization as we know it today was the simple listing of martyrs and their place of burial in the *Kalendarium* or the *Martyrologium,* that is, church-approved calendars or lists of the names of martyrs together with their feast days.

The subsequent evolution of the *Kalendarium* and *Martyrologium* presents an extremely complex, and imperfectly understood, historical process. The general historical lines are relatively clear, however, and give us a good insight into the whole development of the *cultus* of the saints. Professor Hermann Schmidt has provided a good schematic outline of the development and it is from his work that I have borrowed the following abbreviated schema:[2]

1. *The Era of the Ancient Martyrologies.* This period runs from the earliest lists of martyrs we possess to about the seventh century. In this period, we find such early items as a list of the Roman bishops from the fourth century and the ancient fourth-century catalog of Roman martyrs along with their feast days and a list of the places around Rome where they are buried. From this same period, but somewhat later, are martyrologies compiled in Egypt, Carthage, among the Goths, in Jerusalem, and the martyrology of the Syriac Church.

2. *The Early Medieval Martyrologies.* These are lists compiled mainly by monks in the eighth and ninth centuries. In these martyrologies, there were a number of *confessores* (hence, the word *martyrologies* is a bit misleading). There are some martyrs on these lists about whose existence or deeds we have serious historical doubt. These lists were widely used in monastic liturgies. There is a wide range of them, reflecting the predominantly monastic character of the period. Schmidt lists twelve different martyrologies compiled between the time of the English monk, the Venerable Bede (died in 735) and the early eleventh century.

3. *From the Eleventh Century to 1583.* In the medieval period, there was a veritable explosion of saints added to the various extant *Kalendaria* while the number of *Kalendaria* also increased; for example, each of the major religious orders (such as the Cistercians and the Franciscans) began to develop its own lists of saints, especially of those who were venerated *en famille.* Many saints added in the Middle Ages were legendary figures, their names were wrong, or stories about them were conflated beyond recognition. All the early Roman bishops, for example, were given feast days and called "martyrs" even though there was little historical evidence for such a designation for many of them. This period saw a totally undisciplined and fabulous development of lives of the saints.

4. *Publication of the* Martyrologium Romanum *of Pope Gregory*

XIII in 1682. The muddled conditions of these lists in the liturgical calendars of the medieval church led to this work, part of the general liturgical renovation that followed the Counter-Reformation Council of Trent. It utilized the early lists of saints found in the various martyrologies, calendars, sacramentaries, and such to restore order and discipline to the official list of saints to be commemorated in the Roman Catholic Church. This martyrology, in turn, has been the object of continued study and revision down to the present day. The Vatican decree of a few years ago to "demote" Saint George and Saint Christopher is one result of the ongoing historical research being carried out on the saints listed in the martyrology.

Even with this very brief overview of the development of the *Kalendarium* and *Martyrologium,* it is easy to see that in the course of time there was a continuing diminution of the historical perspective. The earliest lists (the catalog of Roman bishops or the martyrologium of the fourth-century Church in Rome) reflected historical personages together with more or less accurate descriptions of the place of their *cultus.* The lists of the Dark Ages and the medieval period are gravely suspect in many aspects as hagiography turned more and more to the fabulous and the legendary. In the post-Reformation era, under the pressure of Protestant criticism and the rise of the historical sciences, there were genuine attempts to purge the *Kalendaria* of unreliable material. This work was greatly advanced by scholarly groups such as the Bollandists and the Maurists, both founded in the seventeenth century, who began the work of historical research into the lives of the saints along scientific and critical lines.

The historical corruption of the biographies of the saints takes many forms and undergoes any number of permutations in the medieval period. In its most basic form, there was the inclusion of people who never existed but who took on a fictionalized *persona* because of the accretion of various stories, legends, and romances attached to real historical events. Examples are quite numerous with respect to the Gospel story of the Passion of Christ. Pontius Pilate, for example, is venerated as a saint in the Ethiopian Coptic church by reason of a legend about his supposed conversion in later life. The unnamed soldier who pierced the side of Christ at Calvary (John 19:34) becomes, in Christian legend, a convert and is given the name Longinus (from Cassius Longinus, one of those who stabbed Caesar?). The women who wept for Jesus on his way to the hill of Calvary (Luke 23:27) gave rise to the legend that one of the women wiped his bloody face and, as a sign of favor, had the face of Christ printed on her towel. The woman of this legend was given the name of Veronica (*Veron Icona*—a "true image"); she is thus named in the devotional practice of the "Stations of the Cross" and the towel she used (the *sudarium*) is still preserved and shown at Saint Peter's Basilica in Rome.

Perhaps the most curious (and most interesting) of this misappropriation of persons into the medieval *cultus* is the case of Saint Josaphat (and the Romance of Josaphat and Barlaam), widely venerated in the Middle Ages though he is, in fact, the Buddha. Evidently a story of the life of the Buddha entered Europe via the trade routes or from returning crusaders and was transformed into a life of an Eastern saint. The Buddha became Saint Josaphat, the name Josaphat most likely a corruption of one of the titles of the Buddha, *Boddhisattva*.

While any number of legendary persons entered the lists of saints in the Middle Ages, far more common was the transformation of a saint's life by the endless weaving of legendary material about the person. One of the most difficult tasks of the scientific hagiographer is trying to unravel the skein of fiction to find what historical material might be hidden in the entire fabric. We would do well to recall the observations of Hippolyte Delehaye, the most famous student of hagiography in this century: "hagiographers do just as poets do: they affect complete independence of, sometimes lordly contempt for, historical facts; for real persons they substitute strongly marked types; they borrow from anywhere in order to give color to their narratives and to sustain interest; above all, they are ever mindful of the marvellous, so apt for heightening the effect of an edifying subject."[3]

One of the most famous instances of this transformation can be seen in the history of Saint Christopher, whose medals are ubiquitous in our culture.[4] Saint Christopher, usually shown as a huge man with staff in hand and a child sitting on his shoulder, adorns automobile dashboards, control panels of boats and planes, and is found around the necks of both pious Catholics and ecumenically minded religious skeptics. He is the patron saint of travelers because the story has it that he once was a ferryman at a river crossing. Medieval folk believed to look on his image was enough to preserve one from death on that day. What, in fact, do we know about this immensely popular saint?

Saint Christopher had widespread *cultus* in the early Eastern Church, where he was venerated as one of the "Fourteen Holy Helpers." There was a church named for him as early as the middle of the fifth century in Constantinople. The oldest martyrologies list him as a martyr who suffered in Asia Minor (Lydia is the place most often named), possibly under the persecution of Diocletian. Modern scholars, given the antiquity of his cult and the allusions in the early martyrologies, are willing to admit there was an unnamed early martyr in Asia Minor who was given the name Christopher. That much is a safe, but not definitive, historical deduction.

To this rather scanty piece of historical fact was added a whole patina of fancy and legend in both the Eastern and Western Church without much internal consistency or reasonability. An early Greek *Vita* says the saint was originally a dog-headed monster who practiced cannibalism, later converted to Christianity, and was martyred. A tenth-century Western *Vita* calls him *Reprobus* (Reprobate), who, upon conversion, took the name *Christopherous*. The famous medieval *Legenda Aurea* of Jacopus da Voragine says he was a giant named Offeros who served, *seriatim*, a barbarian king, the devil, and, upon conversion, Christ. He then became a ferryman and a hermit. He once carried a child across a river. The child was crushingly heavy and Christopher subsequently learned the child was Christ, who carried the sins of the world upon his shoulders. This legend is linked to the saint's name since Christopher in Greek means "The Christ Bearer." The current iconography of the saint, with his staff and the child on his shoulder, derives from this story, which can only be traced back to the Middle Ages. It is interesting, as a parenthetical note, that both Erasmus and Luther thought Saint Christopher was a Christian reworking of the Hercules legend of pagan antiquity.

That this fanciful approach to the saints is not to be explained away by pointing to the credulity of the early medieval mind is clear from the case of "Saint Philomena," whose cult dates only from the nineteenth century.[5] In fact, the case of Philomena aptly illustrates how a lack of clear historical perspective can permit the development of a totally imaginative *cultus*. The relative modernity of this case gives us, as it were, a laboratory example of the development of the imaginary in a saint's *cultus*.

In 1802, Don Francesco DiLucia, a parish priest from the town of Mugnano near Naples, obtained some relics from Rome to enshrine in his home church. These relics had been recently recovered from the cemetery of Priscilla. A tomb had been found in those catacombs with the inscription *Lumena-Paxte-Fi*. A glass vial was found in the tomb along with some bones, thought to be those of a young girl. The conventional wisdom of the time had it that the inscription was to be read as saying "Philomena, peace be with you" and that the vial contained some of the martyr's blood. Don DiLucia not only installed the remains from the tomb in his church at Mugnano but, to increase devotion, wrote a life of the saint with the usual imaginative baggage of hagiography: The young girl refused marriage to a pagan youth and was, as a consequence, denounced to the authorities, tortured with various cruel refinements, and finally executed.

The *cultus* of Saint Philomena spread with amazing rapidity. A famous and influential Catholic laywoman, Pauline Jaricot (who founded, among other things, the Society of the Propagation of the Faith), claimed to have been cured of her various grievous illnesses while making a pilgrimage to the shrine from France. Saint John Vianney, the famous Curé d'Ars (later canonized and made patron saint of all parish priests) was an assiduous promotor of Saint Philomena's cult in France. The Holy See permitted the composition of a Mass and liturgical office in her honor for use in the public worship of the Church. Many parishes assumed Saint Philomena as their patroness, and the name became a popular baptismal one for

Italian girls both in the last century and in this one.

The beginning of the *cultus* of Saint Philomena in 1802 just barely antedates the beginnings of the science of Christian archaeology, which got its start in Rome due to the indefatigable labors of the Jesuit historian, Father Marchi, and the Roman lay scholar and autodidact (he was a lawyer by profession), Giovanni B. de Rossi.[6] Their researches, and that of subsequent scholars, brought about a completely new understanding of the catacombs and their relationship to the early persecutions. Together with the knowledge and a better appreciation of early Roman epigraphy and early Christian art history, it became much easier to understand what tombs in the catacombs actually held the bodies of martyrs (in fact, none of them did since the known martyrs were exhumed and reburied inside the Roman walls in the seventh and eighth centuries during the time of the Barbarian invasions) and how to identify those tombs.

What is clear from these researches is that the inscription of the tomb in question was mistranslated (except for the *"Paxte"*—Peace be with you—it is untranslated; the "philomena" might simply be an adjective meaning "beloved one"), and there is no epigraphical evidence that the dead person was a martyr. The vial was a commonplace object put into many tombs (it is found in Jewish cemeteries of the same period) and has no connection with martyrdom. In fact, the evidence points to a contrary conclusion. The tombs of martyrs were clearly designated as such. In short, the cult of "Saint Philomena" began with a simple historical misunderstanding and developed through the activities of overheated religious imaginations. The evidence was so clear in this instance that the Vatican abolished the *cultus* of Saint Philomena in April 1961 and removed her name from the *Martyrologium.*

The foregoing examples have been provided (and their number could be multiplied a hundredfold) not to expose religious credulity in the spirit of the debunker. It is more a case of underscoring the entangled problems of historicity in the whole development of the *cultus* of the saints. The twin problems of authenticity (Was there such a person?) and historicity (Are the things written about this saint true?) have been of interest to the Church for centuries. The reason is obvious. Incredulity about the saints damages the very credibility of the Church since it is the Church that proposes the saints for the veneration of the public. It is for this reason the Church found it necessary to develop (slowly, to be sure) a procedure that would, as it were, certify the saint. This procedure—canonization—has had a long and tortuous development in the history of the Western Church.[7]

As one surveys the historical development of the formal canonization process, two things become quite clear. First, the process was needed to ensure that the cult of the saints was a dignified one. This was a clear need since the saints were so closely identified with the liturgical life of the Church. It was simply undesirable that that liturgical and paraliturgical life of the Church be outside its control. There is an ancient aphorism in Christianity that the life of worship is the life of faith *(lex orandi, lex credendi)*, and history records how bitterly the Church has fought on occasion to keep the life of worship from being tainted either with heterodox belief or inappropriate expression. Since the saints were venerated in the Church, the Church felt a compelling need to halt the multiplication of feasts of local saints with dubious credentials in the various calendars of Christian Europe.

A second result of the development of formal canonization procedures has been less beneficial but equally noteworthy. By establishing criteria and procedures for determining who would be liturgically recognized in the worship life of the Church, there was a built-in censorship mechanism that would permit the Church to promote or suppress certain personalities together with the images they protected according to the perceived need of the Church. There is a vast volume yet to be written on the sociology of canonizations in the Catholic tradition. Such a study might well show that certain persons appear in the list of the canonized for very particular and apparent political or social reasons. One should not underestimate the apologetic possibilities in the canonization process itself.

Until the tenth century, saints were proclaimed by the simple device of listening to the *vox populi,* even though there are instances where local bishops carried the power of veto over a particular *cultus* in their area of competence. In general, if the people of a particular area wanted to venerate a certain person who had a reputation of being a miracle worker, the cult would spring up rather spontaneously and Church authorities would nurture and protect the cult. From the tenth to the thirteenth century, this spontaneous "canonization of the saints" (note that the word "canonization" meant simply the putting of a saint on an approved "list" or *canon*) was increasingly modified by ecclesiastical intervention. First by custom and then by law, it became usual for the local bishop to read out an account of the saint's life (the original meaning of the word "legend" was something that was read aloud; from the Latin *legere,* to read) together with a proclamation of the saint's miracles. On that same occasion, permission was given to exhume the saint's body and move it to a shrine location (the so-called *translatio*) for public veneration. This process of translation was often done with great solemnity. Miracles and prodigies were expected to occur at the time of the solemn removal of a saint's body to its shrine. Hence, along with the *legenda* of the saint's lives there also arose a subgenre of hagiography, the *translatio,* that is, the accounts of the prodigies that happened on the occasion of the transfer of the saint's body from one place to another.

The earliest documented case of a local saint being proclaimed as such from the papal altars was that of a Saint Uldaricus in 973 during the reign of Pope Benedict VI. In order to give greater solemnity to the public proclamation of the worthiness of a saint, it became more and more common for the bishops to request the popes to proclaim the saints and to order the *translatio* of their relics. In 1234, the period of the apex of papal power, Pope Gregory IX reserved the right of canonization for the papacy alone.

The process of canonization was more minutely regulated as part of the general liturgical and jurisprudential reform of Catholicism during the period of the Counter-Reformation. Pope Sixtus V established the Sacred Congregation of Rites in 1588 as the agency for the canonization of saints. The actual procedures for canonization were further elaborated by Pope Urban VIII in 1642 and by Pope Benedict XIV, who, based on his extensive experience before becoming pope as a member of the Roman Curia, published the influential *De*

Servorum Dei Beatificatione et Beatorum Canonizatione ("On the Beatification of Servants of God and Their Canonization") in 1734. This treatise, in four huge folio volumes, has been extremely influential in the whole juridical process of canonization in the modern Church. It is still the *point du depart* for the canonization procedures of the contemporary Church.

In our own century, there have been further developments at the curial level. Pope Pius X divided the Congregation of Rites into two distinct competencies: one to monitor liturgical law and the other devoted solely to the canonization of saints. In 1930, Pope Pius XI added a historical section to the congregation. Recent reforms of the Vatican Curia (initiated by the late Pope Paul VI as a result of the reforms of Vatican II) have brought further modifications. Currently, the canonization process is under the jurisdiction of the Sacred Congregation for the Causes of the Saints. This Office is charged with the beatification and canonization of saints as well as the preservation and authentication of relics.

The actual process of canonization generally follows the procedures set by Pope Benedict XIV in the eighteenth century. The procedural steps in the canonization process can be summarized briefly:[8]

1. If a person is of reputed heroic sanctity, a preliminary inquiry can be made into his or her life and deeds by the local bishop. This "ordinary" or "informative" process gathers evidence of sanctity, facts about the person's utterances and writings to ensure doctrinal orthodoxy, and any cases of reputed miracles done through the intercession of that person. This material is synthesized into a dossier and forwarded to the Sacred Congregation in Rome.

2. The dossiers prepared at the local level are studied and augmented by the *postulator* of the person under scrutiny. The postulator advances his proofs about the heroic sanctity of the person. His case is studied and challenged by the Defender of the Faith (the *Defensor Fidei* is the famous "devil's advocate"), who makes his objections. When these are satisfactorily answered, a completed document (the *Positio*) is prepared and then discussed by the

prelates and cardinals of the congregation. Their recommenda-
tions are made known to the pope. If there is an affirmative
recommendation, the pope then decrees the "Introduction of the
Cause." At this point, the whole process comes directly under the
authority of the Vatican and is now considered an "Apostolic
Process."

3. A formal scrutiny of the life and deeds of the "servant of God"
is now initiated and a series of documents is prepared concerning
the life and deeds of the persons to be canonized. The usual
dialectical procedure between the postulator and the Defender of
the Faith is carried on even at this level. The last of the formal
inquiries is made with the pope present; and if the judgment about
the person is favorable (and the requisite miracles are in evidence),
the pope declares the person beatified. That person now enjoys
the title of "Blessed." The rite of beatification means the person
may be venerated publicly in the local church but not in the
universal Church. The *cultus* of the "Blessed" is restricted to a
particular locality or within the confines of a particular religious
order.

4. When the localized cult of a beatified person has produced more
evidence of miracles, the final stage may be reached: canonization.
The canonization of a saint consists of the pope's public declaration of the person to be a saint. This is usually done amid the
pageantry of Saint Peter's with the pope affirming that the *Beatus*
is indeed a saint, worthy of veneration, powerful in intercession,
and a model of Christian virtue. The *cultus* of the new saint can
now be extended to the entire Church and the saint's name is
included in the liturgical calendar of the universal Church.

This complex, slow, and convoluted process of canonization is
cumbersome, coldly juridical, and highly stylized. It is a process that
has had a long evolution. It enjoys the force of law since the process,
in its main lines, is prescribed in the Code of Canon Law, which
contains the procedural law of Roman Catholicism. With the proposed revision of Canon Law now well under way, it is possible that
the present machinery will be overhauled or drastically modified in

the future better to reflect contemporary exigencies and sensibilities. At this point, we have no assurance of such changes; they can only be anticipated.

The present canonization process has served the Church well by providing some kind of "quality control" over those who will enjoy the public recognition of the liturgical calendar. Had there been a similar rigorous process in the Middle Ages, we might have been spared some of the less edifying personalities that have found their place in the cycle of saints. The very length of the canonization process (normally the process does not begin until fifty years after the death of the person, but this requirement is on occasion waived) helps the Church get some historical perspective on the persons of reputed sanctity whose causes are brought before them. We can find some small consolation that today persons who dishonor the name of Christianity by prejudice or bigotry will not find their way into the calendar, as they obviously did in the past (such as anti-Semites like Saint Vincent Ferrer or King Saint Louis or rigid fanatics like Pope Saint Pius V).

I suggested in Chapter 1 that one very serious imbalance in the canonization process has been the lopsided emphasis on the miraculous. The thaumaturgic element, understandable in the evolution of the Church, might well be an anachronism in many ways. A good case could be made for saying that the miraculous is only *per accidens* a characteristic of heroic sanctity and as such should be treated as an element that could well suffer a bit of benign neglect. At any rate, the relationship of the miraculous to the heroically holy needs some radical rethinking if the whole notion of the saint is not to be undervalued or trivialized by the modern Christian.

Beyond the problematical question of the role of the miraculous in understanding the authentic notion of sanctity, there are a number of other difficulties for the modern sensitive Christian that arise, as a by-product, from the canonization process itself. The gradual change from the canonization by will of the *vox populi* to canonizations done by a carefully rationalized process is a classic example of the force of bureaucratization at work. What was once done by popular zeal, impetuosity, sentiment, and enthusiasm (with all their attendant aberrations) was done after the thirteenth century by investigation, analysis, dialectic, and, to be sure, with prudential judgments of a politically and socially sensitive Church. In rare instances, the personality of the saint was such that the process was completed with haste (Saint Francis was canonized two years after his death), but that was not generally the case. As in most Vatican affairs, the canonization process exemplifies the old Italian proverb to perfection: *chi va piano, va sano e lontano*—whoever goes slowly, goes far and in good health.

The bureaucratization of sainthood (the word "bureaucratic" is used descriptively, not pejoratively; it derives in the Weberian sense from the process of rationalization) has resulted in a number of grave deficiencies, deficiencies that have lessened both interest in and credibility of the saints. In many ways, these deficiencies are a microcosm of the defects now being addressed in that whole process of renovation in the Church that is called *Aggiornamento.* Any fair and impartial student of the subject of saints would agree, it seems to me, that the very process of canonization tends to produce saints for our veneration who are outside the interests of the average intelligent modern Christian. It could be argued, in fact, that the almost total decline of interest in the subject of saints—apart from a certain residual sentimentality or loyalty to the old forms—can be traced to a quiet rebellion of the modern mind against the roster of saints that has been bequeathed to us as a result of the bureaucratization of the saints.[9] After all, how often does one hear sermons about the virtues of the saints? How many theologians write about the saints or reflect on their place in the life of the Church? Why is there a dearth of decent hagiography in the bookstores today? What does the word "saint" conjure up in the mind of the average Christian? In fact, even in Catholic circles, there seems to be a bifurcated attitude in which there exists a neglected official list of saints and those contemporary heroes of the faith who, in fact, attract the attention and the idealism of the modern Catholic. While comparisons are invidious, one can ask whether, say, Saint Elizabeth Seton means as much to the modern Catholic as does, for example, Dorothy Day or Mother Teresa of Calcutta.

What, specifically, are the most patent weaknesses and deficiencies that have arisen from the bureaucratic control of the canonization of saints in the Roman Catholic Church? First, and most glaringly, is the almost total clericalization of the calendar of saints. This fact can be clearly seen by a simple examination of the roster of saints commemorated in any random month in the Roman rite of the Catholic Church. In the month of March, for example, there are only three nonclerics in the Roman calendar. March 6 is the feast of Saint Perpetua and Saint Felicity; March 9, of Saint Francesca Romana (who, it should be noted, spent the last seven years of her life as a Benedictine oblate); and on March 19, the feast of Saint Joseph is celebrated. In the month of May—apart from some early martyrs whose status is unclear—the only nonclerical saint is the redoubtable mother of Saint Augustine, Saint Monica.

This clericalization of the liturgical calendar must be understood, at least from the end of the Middle Ages, as not only reflecting a clerical bias but consisting almost entirely of clerics from religious orders or nuns from female orders. Apart from certain exceptions in the ranks of the higher clergy (bishops or popes), this is a safe and almost total generalization. To go back again to the month of May, one finds there are seven saints born after 1500 (in the Reformation and post-Reformation period) commemorated in that month. One is a pope who had been a Dominican priest (the unlovely Pius V); four were members of religious orders; and two were founders of new religious orders. There are no laypersons, no diocesan priest, and only one female religious (the Florentine mystic and Carmelite, Maria Magdalena de'Pazzi). In June, there are four saints commemorated who were born after 1500; all are Italian members of religious orders. Neither month is atypical of the calendar as a whole. In fact, one could argue, with a certain whimsical edge, that a quick perusal of the Church calendar of saints would lead one to define a modern saint as any conspicuously pious European who happens to have founded a new religious order after the Reformation.

On a more serious level, it is easy to see how such a clerical overloading of the calendar came about. At the level of the theoretical, there was the idea, deeply rooted in Catholic piety and doctrine, that the vowed life of the religious was the more perfect form of the Christian life since it was the religious who followed the "evangelical counsels" (or, as they were called, "the counsels of perfection") of poverty, chastity, and obedience. Thus, the vowed religious was more clearly and "professionally" committed to the pursuit of perfection. The Church expected perfection from the religious orders. It was the Reformation that reacted against this division of classes in the Church; one may recall Max Weber's *mot* that after the Reformation, everybody was called to be a monk. Only more recently have we clearly distinguished between the "Evangelical Counsels" in the canonical sense (that is, Religious Life as defined in the Code of Canon Law) and the Evangelical Counsels as demands on every baptized Christian to put on more fully the life of Christ. In the latter sense, obviously, everyone is called upon to seek the life of perfection.

In the intense discussions about the meaning of the "counsels of perfection" going on today both in and outside of religious orders, we shall see wider and less-juridical understandings of these ideas. As that happens, the limited value of the older calendar of the liturgical year will become all the more clear. The increasing unwillingness of the people of the Church to be "second-class citizens" or to be categorized as simply the "laity" is not only a fact of life today but derives, in its most authentic manifestation, from the clear teaching of the Fathers of Vatican II. The very development of an adequate understanding of the implications of the Council on the Priesthood of the Laity, for example, is quickly reducing the traditional calendar of the saints to historical curiosity.

If my contention that canonization is a bureaucratic process is correct, then one can find in that fact another reason members of religious orders came to such prominence in the calendar of saints. The religious orders had the structures ready to "plug in" to the bureaucratic process. If a layperson were of eximious piety, the local diocese would have to initiate the lengthy and costly process of inquiry; and then, at the curial level, there would be need of a postulator and someone to oversee the apostolic process. This is a demandingly lengthy and costly process. Religious orders, by contrast, not only had the expertise at hand (many of the larger orders have historical institutes with trained scholars attached to them), but are usually permanently represented in Rome through their mother-house or generalate. Beyond that, the religious orders have the finan-cial resources (no small irony here!) to undertake the process itself. To put the matter most specifically, the Franciscans have the money, resources, and expertise to further the cause of any holy friar; but one finds it hard to think of an anarchical and improvident group like the Catholic Workers using their funds for the canonization of someone like Peter Maurin, despite the fact that he might be the most Francis-can personality of the Western Church in the modern period.

There is nothing inherently repugnant about an overly generous sprinkling of vowed religious in the calendar of saints, except that their life-style is not that of most Christians. They tend to edify not the faithful at large but that segment of the faithful who have the closest ties to the bureaucracy that puts forward the saints. Their number represents not the reality of Christian life and its possibilities but certain sociological trends in historical Christianity. It is impor-tant to keep such contingent distortions in mind if one is to assess the limitations of the "formal" tradition of saints.

Another unhappy by-product of the bureaucratization of the saint's calendar is that when the calendar is viewed *in globo,* it tends to reflect many other prejudices that have arisen as the result of past historical contingencies. The matter of sexual stereotyping is one glaring example of this prejudice. It is true that the one area of ecclesiastical honor that is open to male and female alike is the right to be considered officially a saint and receive the honors that accrue to that title. The ancient Church gives many ready symbolic exam-ples of this area of egalitarianism: The parallel listing of male and female martyrs in the canon of the Roman rite of the Mass is one famous example. At a more visual level, one can point to the great mosaic in the fifth-century Church of San Appolinare Nuovo in Ravenna where, on opposite sides of the nave of the basilica, equal rows of male and female martyrs walk in solemn procession toward the apse of the church. In a more recent small gesture of equality, two female saints have been named as "Doctors of the Church"; now Saint Teresa of Avila and Saint Catherine of Siena join such theological luminaries as Saint Augustine of Hippo, Saint Thomas Aquinas, and Saint Bernard of Clairvaux.

With that minor affirmation of equality in mind, one should note some extremely distasteful anomalies in the classification of saints in the Roman calendar. A schema that Hermann Schmidt provides is instructive in this regard.[10] The three basic liturgical classifications of saints are martyrs, confessors, and virgins. This basic tripartite classification has been enlarged to include such subcategories as pope, abbot, founder, apostle, evangelist, and doctor. There may even be a combination of titles like "pope-martyr" or "confessor-founder." One classification that catches the modern eye is that of the "non-virgin" *(non-virgo)*.[11] No men are put into this classification. Of all the women so classified, some are also martyrs (like Saint Perpetua and Saint Felicity) or founders (Saint Jane Frances de Chantal), but married women (Saint Monica or Elizabeth of Hungary) are simply non-virgins or widows. One can raise the question about the world view that undergirds such a division. Saint Augustine of Hippo (feast day on August 28) is listed as a "confessor-doctor-bishop" but not a nonvirgin, which he certainly was if one can credit the testimony of the *Confessions.*

The previous example, petty in a certain way, is but a symptom of the celibate mentality and the sexual prejudice of the catalog of the saints. Except for the early martyrs and popes (whose marital status is, at times, hard to determine), the *Kalendarium* gives short shrift to those Christians who are married, as if that less-perfect state somehow disqualifies from public recognition of sanctity. The exaggeration of celibate values is familiar to anyone who has looked at a good deal of traditional hagiography. In the second nocturns of the older Roman breviary, one finds a treasure trove of examples of sexual prejudice and odd exaltations of celibate values.

Paging through the breviary at random, one finds many instances of this antisexual attitude. At the risk of belaboring an obvious point, let me cite some examples chosen from the August calendar of the cycle of saints. On August 17, Saint Hyacinth is praised for keeping his virginity intact throughout his entire life *(virginitate perpetuo intacta)*.[12] Saint John Eudes on August 19 is described as having made a vow of perpetual chastity while he was still a child *(adhuc puer perpetuam castitatem vovit)*. Saint Jane Frances de Chantal (August 21) not only vowed perpetual chastity after the death of her husband but also sealed this vow—this should give amateur Freudians some pause—by burning the name of Jesus on her breast with a hot iron *(Jesu Christi nomen candenti ferro suo pectori insculpsit)*. Saint Rose of Lima on August 30 is praised for avoiding the snare of marriage by shaving her head.

One final limitation of the present canonization process deserves more particular attention. That is the test of doctrinal orthodoxy. Before the Roman Congregation will even consider the cause of a saint, the local bishop must undertake a thorough scrutiny of the candidate's utterances to ensure there is no record of deviation from the standards of Roman Catholic orthodoxy. The standard of orthodoxy, in the modern Church, is that formulation of faith represented by the Profession of Faith of the Council of Trent or, more recently, the antimodernist Profession of Faith or the Credo of the People of God (of Pope Paul VI). In practice, not only orthodoxy but freedom from any critical spirit is also demanded of the candidate. This might explain why many famous mystics (one thinks of Meister Eckhart, Richard Rolle, and Julian of Norwich) have never been canonized. It also explains the absence of preeminently holy persons who were ensnared in ecclesiastical controversy (such as Blaise Pascal) or someone who has formulated Catholic doctrine in an unusual or new way. Thus, it is unlikely that Antonio Rosmini-Serbati (1795–1855), a man of undoubted sanctity and fidelity to the Church and a founder of a religious order, will be easily advanced for canonization since some of his books were placed on the Index in the last century. One of those books (*Delle cinque piaghe della chiesa,* placed on the Index in 1849) is a prophetic call for more democracy in the Church and is, by today's standards, benign. Likewise, Pierre Teilhard de Chardin, a paradigmatic Christian and mystic of the utmost probity, would have to pass insuperable hurdles in the canonical process due to the novelty of his expression and the extreme suspicion of the Roman Curia about his theological speculations.

It could be argued with complete plausibility that both Rosmini and Teilhard de Chardin should receive the public acclaim of the Church precisely because they were, at the same time, extremely faithful Catholic Christians and pioneers who sought new ways to express the faith in a manner congruent with the age in which they lived. In other words, the test should not be some narrow definition of doctrinal orthodoxy but a judgment about the nobility of the attempt to be faithful to the Gospel and the strenuousness with which the person attempts to present that Gospel to a world yet to be evangelized.

The problem of doctrinal orthodoxy becomes all the more problematical when one puts it in the context of the declaration of the Second Vatican Council, especially the *Decree on Ecumenism* and the *Declaration on Non-Christian Religions*. In the light of the teaching and spirit of Vatican II, it is a commonplace, indeed, a doctrinal truth, that sanctity of a heroic kind can exist outside the bounds of Roman Catholicism. Beyond such a theoretical statement, one can see evidences of heroic virtue and sanctity among those who were openly outside the Roman Catholic Church; John Wesley comes immediately to mind. Twenty years ago the English writer John Todd suggested the canonization of Wesley as an ecumenical gesture. Our own lamentable history of war and persecution has produced genuine martyrs for the sake of Christ (such as Dietrich Bonhoeffer) who were not Roman Catholics. Many of these persons were not only personally holy but led paradigmatic lives; they taught useful new ways of incarnating the Christian message into real life. In the common estimation, these people are saints; in these cases, it is the *vox populi* that has spoken. Yet, given the current dispensation, it is unlikely they will reach the altars of the Church. One can only speculate on the ecumenical worth of reversing this procedure so a Wesley or a Bonhoeffer could be listed in the canon of the saints. The problem becomes more acute when one begins to think of those who have been canonized by the *vox populi* as saints but who are perceived as heterodox (Albert Schweitzer) or only influenced by Christianity (Gandhi).

Indeed, it can be argued that the Catholic Church has used the canonization process as an instrument of bureaucratic control to ensure compliance with their ideal of doctrinal and spiritual conformity. This has been recognized by social scientists who have worked with institutional sociology. Amitai Etzioni, for example, has argued that the Catholic Church (like the Communist party) has employed canonization as a mechanism to turn deviant charismatic symbols into a focus of conforming identification. By reinterpreting the image of the deviant leader, the Church rechannels devotion to the charismatic symbol to the organization and its goals. The canonization of Saint Joan of Arc is probably the best-known example.[13] Etzioni continues, "Canonization is a dangerous mechanism. If used widely and freely it may encourage deviance because it grants the deviant hope of becoming a saint. The Church has special safety devices against this possibility: No one can become a saint until fifty years after death, and extensive tests are required before a person is recognized as a saint. A deviant can hardly count on sainthood."[14]

The formal canonization process, needed in given historical circumstances, is a reflection of a clericalized culture in the process of rapid disintegration in our own time. It does not respond to the exigencies of our day, a day that has a great thirst for the holy and an admiration for those who can hold that ideal before us. My contention (argued at length later in this book) is that the whole business of canonization as we have it today in the Church is largely irrelevant and should be abandoned or radically modified. The recognition of sanctity should be, in fact, is, the result of the *vox populi*.

The proposal to abandon or emarginate the formal canonization process is not as radical or destructive as it might appear at first glance. Canonization procedures as they now exist were established to fulfill a particular need at a particular time in the history of Christianity. They were established not to determine who was a saint but which saints were to have public cultic honors in the Church. Canonization is linked very closely to cult. It seems evident that the contemporary experience of the saint is not found primarily in their veneration but in their function as exemplars.

In Western Catholicism, the liturgical cult of the saints is in a state of seemingly inexorable decline. The commemorative feasts of saints have either been trivialized into folk feasts (think of Saint

Valentine's day in this country) or symbolic expressions of passions only minimally religious (such as Saint Patrick's Day) or feast days of an apologetic bent with little relevance outside narrowly national boundaries (the feast of Saint Joseph the worker is celebrated on May 1 in Italy as an "antidote" to the Communist May Day celebrations). Beyond such public expressions, "Saint's Days" tend to be the province of various religious orders or particular locales. It is interesting that among the proposed changes in the Code of Canon Law is a Church rule that restricts all official Holydays to the Sundays of the year, the feast of Christmas, and one day in honor of the Blessed Virgin Mary.[15]

Private devotion to the saints has likewise been in eclipse in modern Catholicism. While it is still possible to see ads in Catholic papers recommending the intercessory powers of various saints with miraculous powers, such enthusiasms seem marginal to the life of most Christians. It was perhaps inevitable that the orientation of postconciliar Catholicism—with its strong emphasis on biblical, liturgical, and theological matters—should act as a strong agent for the decline of less-sophisticated forms of devotion.

Curiously enough, at the precise time when interest in the intercessory or cultic power of the saints is in some decline, there has been a corresponding interest in religious figures as paradigms. The current interest in the theological dimensions of story, biography, autobiography, and personal narrative has turned to a renewed interest in the saintly personality. Likewise, the *vox populi* in this regard can be seen in the unusually eclectic range of figures who have caught the eye of the religiously literate. The contemporary scene reveals any number of institutes and religious centers named for such popular and uncanonized figures as Pope John XXIII, M. Gandhi, Martin Luther King, Jr., Thomas Merton, and Albert Schweitzer. In a rather inspired choice, one Christian activist group near Washington, D.C., has called itself "Quixote Center." Don Quixote was a fictional character, but the value of his *persona* as a model is recognized. The activists who made this choice are in very good company. Countless churches and ecclesiastical centers are named for saints who are fictional characters, that is, they are products of the hagiographical imagination. What the members of the Quixote Center are doing by their choice of a patron is to proclaim the religious "style" with which they wish to identify: a profoundly compassionate idealism that appears to the world to be, well, quixotic.

Any deemphasis of the ecclesiastical canonization process would be a generous ecumenical gesture. It would symbolize dramatically the presence of heroic sanctity outside the visible parameters of Roman Catholicism. The *vox populi* of the entire Christian community could then give their equal approbation to a Pastor Bonhoeffer and a Maximilian Kolbe as well as a Gandhi or a Schweitzer. It would be to recognize in a concrete way that the call to salvation is a universal one and that the signs of God's grace appear in the midst of all the peoples and cultures of the world. Such a recognition would provide a vivid and concrete expression of the intentions of the Second Vatican Council. If Gandhi could call one of his early *ashrams* Tolstoy Farm, is it mere sentimentality to hope there might be a Christian center called Gandhi House?

The formal process of canonization does certify that the saint is a worthy intercessor. Is that fact an insuperable ecumenical problem if we wish—as we most surely do—to encourage the non–Roman Catholic or Orthodox Christian world to take the saint with seriousness?

The Protestant theologian James W. McClendon has made some tentative suggestions in this area that bear consideration.[16] McClendon proposes, first of all, that Evangelical churches neither condemn nor forbid the practice of intercessory prayers. The Catholic tradition, in turn, should not positively and formally encourage it, "leaving it to each Christian consciousness to learn whether such devotions pass the test proposed here—that is, whether they encourage or rival true devotion to and worship of the Creator."[17] McClendon then goes on to propose that the word "prayer" be reserved for exchanges with God alone since "prayer" and "God" are so closely tied together in the common vocabulary of Christendom.

What of the long-standing tradition of invoking the Blessed Virgin Mary and the other saints in the formal liturgical worship of the Catholic Church? Such invocations could be retained, but they would be linked not to intercessory prayer but to the doctrine of the Communion of the Saints. McClendon suggests, to cite one example, that the *Confiteor* should not read "I confess to Almighty God, *to* Blessed Mary ever Virgin" but "I confess to almighty God *in the presence of* Blessed Mary ever Virgin." The suggestion is a fecund one; it is consistent with current usage in the Roman liturgy. In the Eucharistic Prayer of the Latin Liturgy, for example, we pray "in union with the whole Church" and in that unison we "honor Mary . . . Joseph . . . the Apostles and Martyrs"; in the postconsecration part of that same prayer, we request a "share in the fellowship of your Apostles and Martyrs." Both phrases are clearly oriented to a recognition of our bond with the saints in heaven and our own hope to share in that same status. This recognition of the Communion of the Saints underscores in a dramatic manner the profoundly eschatological character of Christianity.

Would the abandonment of some formal canonization process in the Catholic Church lead to the intolerable anarchy of the early medieval period where "saints" sprang up from the fertile imagination of the hagiographers like so many spring mushrooms? One would have to be a *naif* to deny such a possibility. We live in an age, as Andy Warhol once noted, where everybody can be a celebrity for ten minutes. Religious celebrities are no exception to this rule. We have been gulled by flocks of specious gurus, healers, Hot Gospel money managers, and sundry other charlatans and montebanks who have traded on their reputation for holiness and spiritual probity. There is no evidence that canonization inquiries do much to alleviate this problem.

To recognize the true saint may require the same grace-full eye that one must possess to distinguish the true prophet from the false one. No set of guidelines can ensure such vision, but it is not impossible to sketch out the characteristics one should be looking for in the saint. Such a profile (one I set out in the next chapter) may keep us from quick false judgments. Beyond that, we can only apply the wisdom of Rabbi Gamiliel (Acts 5:38): If the putative saint is of God, he or she will endure; if not, the judgment of time and history will right the matter.

NOTES

1. Many examples can be found in Orazio Marucchi, *Christian Epigraphy*, trans. J. Armine Willis (Chicago: Ares, 1964), p. 439. For such graffiti at the tomb of Saint Peter in Rome, see Margherita Guarducci, *La tomba di Pietro* (Rome: Editrice Studium, 1959), p. 87–139.

2. Hermanus A. P. Schmidt, *Introductio in Liturgiam Occidentalem* (Rome: Herder, 1960), pp. 528–685. For a more recent review of the research with a good bibliography, see Kevin Donovan, "The Sanctoral." In Cheslyn Jones et al., ed., *The Study of the Liturgy* (New York: Oxford University Press, 1978), pp. 419–431.

3. Hippolyte Delehaye, *The Legends of the Saints*, trans. Donald Attwater (New York: Fordham University Press, 1962), p. xviii. This book is a fundamental work for any student of hagiography.

4. For brief biographies of the saints, consult any of the following: Benedictine Monks of Saint Augustine Abbey, ed., *The Book of Saints* (New York: Crowell, 1921); Alban Butler, ed. *Lives of the Saints*, reedited by Herbert Thurston, S. J. and Donald Attwater 4 vols. (New York: Kenedy, 1956); *The Penguin Dictionary of Saints*, Donald Attwater, ed. (London: Penguin Books, 1965); and the various entries in *The New Catholic Encyclopedia*. 15 vols. (New York: McGraw Hill, 1967). I found useful (especially for its good material on iconography and its bibliographies) *Biblioteca Sanctorum*. 12 vols. (Rome: Istituto Giovanni XXIII, 1961)—in Italian.

5. See "Philomena." In *New Catholic Encyclopedia*, vol. II, p. 292.

6. The story is well told in L. Hertling and E. Kirschbaum, *The Roman Catacombs*, trans. M. Joseph Costelloe (Milwaukee: Bruce, 1960).

7. See Paolo Molinari, "Canonization." In *New Catholic Encyclopedia*, vol. 3, pp. 55–59, for a summary and, more succinctly, the same author's entry in *Sacramentum Mundi: An Encyclopedia of Theology*, vol. 5 (New York: Herder and Herder, 1970), pp. 401–402. Both articles have extensive bibliographies.

8. Molinari, "Canonization." The procedures are also spelled out in the *Codex Juris Canonici*, canons 1999–2141.

9. One small example of this disinterest is that nowhere in the index of Hans Küng's monumental *On Being a Christian* is there an entry under the word "saint"; those saints who are mentioned are, with the sole exception of Saint Francis of Assisi, theologians like Saint Augustine or Saint Thomas Aquinas. Hans Küng, *On Being a Christian* (Garden City: Doubleday, 1976). Karl Rahner's recent *Grundkurs*, alas, has no index; but none of the subheadings mention the saints. Karl Rahner, *Foundations of the Christian Faith* (New York: Seabury, 1978).

10. Schmidt, *Introductio in Liturgiam Occidentalem*, pp. 585–605.

11. A subdivision of which is *Vidua*, that is, a "widow"; there is not a corresponding classification for widower.
12. All citations are from the old Roman Breviary in the places indicated.
13. Amitai Etzioni, *A Comparative Analysis of Complex Organizations* (New York: Free Press, 1961), p. 243.
14. Ibid. Note that the fifty-year rule can be waived and has been in such cases as the canonization of Pope Pius X in this century.
15. On the proposed revisions of Canon Law, see Thomas J. Green, "Revision of Canon Law," *Theological Studies* (December 1979), pp. 593–679. It is interesting that this voluminous survey makes no mention of the revision of canonical procedures for canonization. In fact, the subject of saints is not even mentioned.
16. James William McClendon, *Biography As Theology: How Life Stories Can Remake Today's Theology* (Nashville: Abingdon, 1974), pp. 214–215. In this very interesting book, McClendon has an appendix (pp. 204–215) on "Christian Worship and the Saints"; it is an attempt to see the saints as part of the ecumenical encounter. McClendon's understanding of saints is almost exclusively in terms of their cult; it will be one of my purposes to shift attention away from such an orientation.
17. Ibid., p. 215.

CHAPTER 3

Toward an Understanding of Saints

THE WORD "saint" is used in a bewildering variety of ways in contemporary life: "My mother is a living saint," "When the Saints Go Marching In," "Saint Anthony, pray for us," "Albert Camus was a secular saint." The dictionary helps us a bit by providing us with four general categories of the accepted usage of the word: (1) godly people, (2) those Blessed Ones who are in heaven, (3) those persons publicly recognized for their holiness by the process of canonization in the Catholic Church, and (4) the justified, as opposed to the unregenerate, as that distinction is understood in the scriptures of the New Testament. These dictionary descriptions tell us quite a bit and they tell us very little. They adequately categorize popular linguistic usage but provide very little understanding. Such definitions, after all, mirror the canons of ordinary speech. Their purpose is not to provide religious or theological understanding. That is the task of this chapter.

Traditional theology, has been of very little help in providing any systematic reflection on the notion of the saint or the saint's function in Christianity. As Karl Rahner has noted, one must search in the nooks and crannies of the theological manuals even to find any mention of the saints.[1] When such a theological search has been completed, the results are both meager and fragmentary. Saints are discussed in the theology books when the distinction between the worship of God *(latria)* and the veneration of the saints *(dulia)* is made. The process of the canonization of saints is described when the issue is raised of whether or not canonization falls under the charism of papal infallibility. Saints are also mentioned in connection with the doctrine of the Communion of Saints. These theological *obiter dicta* presume the definition of the saint and simply ignore any discussion of the saint's place in the total Christian scheme of things. If one surveys the topics and indexes of any standard theological manual— the exhaustive four-volume *Sacrae Theologiae Summa* published by the Spanish Jesuits on the eve of the Second Vatican Council was my test case—one finds a total lack of attention given to the subject.[2] In this, the manualists in theology are true to their intellectual ancestors since neither the medieval *Summa* nor the Counter-Reformation controversalists devote much energy to the topic. When the late Paul Tillich wrote that a "rethinking of the problem of sainthood by Protestant theology is certainly needed," he could have struck the qualifying adjective "Protestant" without difficulty and substituted the word "Catholic."[3]

On reflection, the paucity of theological consideration of the saints is not hard to explain. The veneration of the saints in the historical tradition of Christianity has been identified with the popular devotional life of the Church. As long as this popular cult did not get out of hand or the legitimacy of it was not impugned, there was little interest in the topic on the part of the theologians or of the ecclesiastical authority. The cult of the saints became the province of the canon lawyer, the hagiographer, or the spiritual writer. The deliberations of the Council of Trent in 1563 (Session XXV) summed up the official Church's attitude succinctly: The invocation of the saints and their intercessory power is an authentic part of Christian tradition. Their bodies and other relics may be venerated and images or pictures of them are a legitimate part of Christian life. It is clear that these dogmatic statements were made to counteract the general Reformation rejection of the veneration of the saints.

This bifurcation of theology and popular devotion has only recently been understood and deplored. The modern liberation theologians are most interested in the popular religiousness of folk Catholicism, since a good deal of Third World Catholicism (most notably in Latin America) has been expressed in popular forms. Any person who has seen the newsreels of striking farm workers marching behind a banner of Our Lady of Guadalupe can appreciate the power of such popular symbols. Popular devotion is close to the personal experience of people; and the current interest in story, biography, spiritual development, and narrative makes it imperative for some sustained reflection on those parts of the Christian tradition that once were dismissed as being unworthy of serious theological reflection.

Beyond the renewed interest of current theology is the striking fact that many people testify to the power of the lives of the saints in their own spiritual development. A recent memoir of growing up in the days of Catholic revival of the 1950s in America makes the point dramatically:

> What mattered, however, was not so much what one did, as what one was. That was, of course, to be a saint. Personal sanctity was the secret of the apostolate, the power which would convert the world. . . .
>
> A new hagiography flourished, breaking the plaster mold in which all the saints seem to have been cast. We were given, instead, holy men and women who had started out life not much different from the rest of us, sometimes even wicked, or worse, mediocre. But through God's grace they abandoned their selfish ways and gave themselves to God in perfect love.[4]

My discussion of the saints will attempt to heal that breach between popular devotion and theological reflection. There are certain presuppositions, implicitly developed in the earlier chapters, I will hold to in my attempt to understand the saint. First of all, we cannot accept the idea that the saint is synonymous with the miracle worker. That is the conclusion of Gerardus van der Leeuw's important phenomenological study, *Religion in Essence and Manifestation.* That equation derives from a past consideration of saints and is, on the face of it, deficient. Our own experience tells us that we use the term saint in a far different way. When we speak of a Mother Teresa of Calcutta as a saint, we do so not because of her thaumaturgic abilities. Nor will I restrict my notion of saints to those who have been formally canonized. Such a restriction is too narrowly juridical;

even the Catholic Church, which employs the juridical process of canonization, does not consider those inscribed in the calendar of the saints as exhausting the witness of heroic sanctity in its own tradition.

In this chapter, I first describe what a saint is and what characteristics best and most aptly illuminate the saintly character. Second, I discuss the ways in which the saintly personality is a value for others, since heroic sanctity is, among other things, a *charism*, that is, a grace for the benefit of others. *A saint is a person so grasped by a religious vision that it becomes central to his or her life in a way that radically changes the person and leads others to glimpse the value of that vision.* This definition is applicable to saints in the Christian tradition. When I say "religious vision," I am implicitly saying "Christian" tradition, although I understand that qualifying "Christian" in the broad sense made possible by the teachings of the Second Vatican Council on the presence of grace outside the visible parameters of institutional Christianity.

I begin with the idea that the saint is "grasped by a religious vision." In *The Varieties of Religious Experience,* William James discusses the idea of saintliness; it is still one of the best treatments of the subject and readers of James will recognize how indebted my discussion is to his chapter on the subject. For James, saintliness can best be described as a habitual state of those who have undergone the powerful transformation of some kind of religious conversion. This radical conversion or transformation ("being grasped by a religious vision") is often called, with varying degrees of sophistication or precision, being "reborn" or becoming a "new person." It is a radical transformation of the person; James writes, "The man who lives in his religious center of personal energy, and is actuated by spiritual enthusiasms, differs from his previous carnal self in perfectly definite ways."[5] This spiritual change is not merely an emotional storm passing over the soul of a person in this or that moment of spiritual enthusiasm or spiritual stress. It is a change that is habitual and produces the deep locus of all subsequent thought and activity.

Is it possible to specify in greater detail the nature of the religious transformation that produces heroic sanctity? James is helpful here; he outlines four characteristics of the religiously transformed:

1. A feeling of being in a wider life than that of this world's selfish little interests; and a corresponding conviction, not merely intellectual, but, as it were, sensible, of the existence of an Ideal Power.
2. A sense of the friendly continuity of the Ideal Power with our own life, and a willing surrender to its control.
3. An immense elation and freedom, as the outlines of the confining selfhood melt down.
4. A shifting of the emotional centre towards loving and harmonious affections, towards "yes, yes" and away from "no" where the claims of the non-ego are concerned.[6]

The religious conversion of the saint may be a dramatic "Road to Damascus" experience, but it need not be; it could be something that evolves slowly in a quiet, internal, or intellectualized manner. The conversion process may come by stages. What is crucial is not the suddenness or the slowness of the transformation; what is crucial is the change that it causes in the person. Whether the conversion is dramatic or not is somewhat irrelevant to its essential nature. What is important is the new affirmation that derives from the transformation, an affirmation, either implied or fully articulated, that radically changes a person's perspective about the self and about others. It can also come in the form of a second conversion, that is, a Christian feels converted to a more perfect pursuit of the Christian vocation. Consider these widely disparate testimonies of religious conversion:

> To me, Brother Francis, the Lord thus gave the grace to do penance: when I was still a sinner I thought it too bitter a thing to look at lepers, and the Lord led me to them and taught me to be merciful. . . . I tarried a bit and then left the world.
>
> (SAINT FRANCIS OF ASSISI, *The Last Testament*)

> God showed me something small, no bigger than a hazelnut, lying in the palm of my hand, and I perceived that it was as round as any ball. I looked at it and thought: what can this be? And I was given the general answer: it is everything which is made. I was amazed that it could last for I thought that it was so little that it could suddenly fall into nothing. And I was answered in my understanding: It lasts and always will, because God loves it; and thus everything has being through the love of God.

In this little thing I saw three properties. The first is that God made it, the second is that He loves it, and the third is that God preserves it.

(JULIAN OF NORWICH, *Showings*)

I discovered the poem of which I read you what is unfortunately a very inadequate translation. It is called "Love" (by George Herbert). I learned it by heart. Often, at the culminating point of a violent headache, I make myself say it over, concentrating all my attention upon it, and clinging with all my soul to the tenderness it enshrines. I used to think I was merely reciting it as a beautiful poem, but without my knowing it the recitation had the virtue of a prayer. It was during one of these recitations, as I told you, Christ himself came down and took possession of me.

(SIMONE WEIL, *Waiting on God*)

In Louisville, at the corner of Fourth and Walnut, in the center of the shopping district, I was suddenly overwhelmed with the realization that I loved all these people, that they were mine, and I theirs, that we could not be alien to one another even though we were total strangers. It was like waking from a dream of separateness, of spurious self-isolation in a special world, the world of renunciation and supposed holiness.

(THOMAS MERTON, *Conjectures of a Guilty Bystander*)

I don't know Who—or what—put the question. I don't know when it was put. I don't even remember answering. But at some moment I did answer YES to Someone—or something—and from that hour I was certain that existence is meaningful and that, therefore, my life, in self-surrender, had a goal.

(DAG HAMMARSKJÖLD, *Markings*)

The year of grace, 1654.
Monday, 23 November, feast of St. Clement, Pope and and Martyr, and of others in the martyrology. Eve of St. Chrysogonus, Martyr and others. From about half past ten in the evening until half past midnight.
    FIRE
"God of Abraham, God of Isaac, God of Jacob" not of philosophers and scholars. Certainty, certainity, heartfelt, joy, peace. God of Jesus Christ.
(From a parchment sewn in the clothing of Blaise Pascal found after his death)

One could multiply these examples from the tradition of spiritual literature. Such testimonies are as old as Abraham's call from "Ur of the Chaldees" to the religious experience of some unknown person who listens for God at this very moment. The experiences reflect different voices, different cultures, and vastly different sensibilities. They do not all represent the beginning of a person's spiritual life. In some cases, they are "second steps" or privileged moments of insight after a long life as a Christian. Thomas Merton had been a Trappist monk for over fifteen years when he had his moment of revelation in downtown Louisville. It was that overwhelming experience of human compassion that caused him to rethink and change his more rigid understanding of monastic vocation. Dag Hammarskjöld penned his "Yes" toward the end of his life, but it is obvious that his affirmation had come some years before. The experiences of Julian of Norwich, Blaise Pascal, and Simone Weil were moments in lives that were already intensely religious. The point being urged here is that saints are not created in a moment. Their road to holiness is not a moment but a process marked by conversional experiences upon which they stake their existence.

Being grasped by a profound religious vision (or what William James calls "Ideal Power") changes the saintly personality by diminishing ego centeredness and creating, as a substitute, what James has called "the feeling of being in a wider life." This diminution of self is a form of asceticism, a characteristic typical of heroic sanctity, according to James. Asceticism is a natural consequence of the religious experience; it flows from it in an almost linear pattern: Religious conversion gives one a wider horizon than the self (a "yes, yes" rather than a "no, no"), and this widening horizon itself engenders a certain asceticism. The deepest balance for the saint is the centrality of the religious vision and the concomitant willingness to sacrifice oneself for that vision; that sacrifice is the ascetic component of sanctity.

To understand this connection between religious vision and asceticism is to understand certain traditional words used in connection with the saint in a fuller and less "pious" way. James notes three in particular. First, saintly asceticism engenders a certain *strength of soul* that provides an antidote to fears and anxieties and produces that equanimity for which the saints are noted. Second, asceticism helps with the development of that goodness that can only be described as *purity*, although the term now has taken on a too narrowly sexual connotation. Finally, there is an increase of self-forgetting *charity* through which the "ordinary motives of antipathy, which usually set such close bounds to tenderness among human beings, are inhibited."[7]

The terms I have used up to this point—words like ideal power, religious vision, asceticism, and purity—lack specificity. They take on specificity only when they are used concretely in a given religious tradition. The rather abstract terms "religious vision" or "ideal power" take on a profoundly personal character in Christianity as the saint feels an intimate relationship with the person of Jesus Christ. Conversely, for a nature mystic like Henry David Thoreau, the ideal power is the undifferentiated power of nature. In a similar manner, the active development of the ideal of asceticism may take on quite different modalities. Asceticism could be seen as a form of discipline as an aid for spiritual awareness (as in Yoga). Asceticism in that instance is quite conscious and something willed. Yet asceticism might simply be the unconscious result of a life dedicated to the serving of others; in that case, it derives not from choice but from self-forgetfulness.

We must be mindful of the fact that the saintly personality can be regarded, by the unsympathetic viewer, as a pathological one. James, after all, was a psychologist; and it was through a psychologist's eyes that he had to view some of the more eccentric manifestations of the saintly personality. Globally viewed, the lives of saintly personalities are so fiercely different that "judging them by worldly law, we might be tempted to call them monstrous aberrations from the path of nature."[8] In any discussion of the saintly personality, one must be sensitive to those boundaries beyond which one finds not authentic sanctity but eccentricity or, more typically, pathology. The most treacherous place to distinguish the true saint from the pathological personality is in the judgment of the ascetical side of the saintly personality.

James felt that asceticism, broadly understood, was a necessary part of the saintly personality. He also recognized that asceticism derives from any number of sources, and some of those sources are suspect. Asceticism may derive from what James has called "organic hardihood"—the revolt against too much self-indulgence or ease (joggers come spontaneously to mind in this regard). It may well up as a desire for greater self-purity emerges or it may come from a deep feeling of love for God. The dark side of asceticism wells up, however, from profoundly pessimistic feelings about the worth of the self (we would call it alienation) or fixated patterns characteristic of the compulsive personality. Finally, there is the inversion of pain into pleasure in which asceticism becomes masochism.

In the matter of asceticism (I emphasize this characteristic because it is the one that gives the modern temper the most worry), a valid rule of thumb would be that asceticism is a healthy phenomenon to the extent that it is a servant of the saintly personality. Once it becomes an end in itself or overshadows the relationship with the "ideal power," it becomes an end in itself and undermines the subjective state crucial for the true saintly personality. James believed (and rightly, in my estimation) that asceticism must be "acknowledged to go with the profounder way of handling the gift of existence."9 Asceticism can enhance the sense of gratefulness one should have for being in the world as one accepts life and being as a gratuitous gift. Any form of asceticism that destroys such a basic sense of gratefulness is aberrational on the face of it.

A cautionary word may not be out of place. The saint *stands out;* the saint is ab-normal. Nor is sanctity any guarantee that the personality is going to be pleasing or wholesome or even attractive. Some saintly personalities—one thinks of Pope John XXIII—are so transparently good (a Roman cab driver once told me that Pope John was loved because everybody wanted to have an uncle just like him) that their lives radiate an almost childlike simplicity. Others have had their lives sanitized by the forces of time and legend. One wonders how many people would welcome the real Saint Francis, in all of his poverty, into their living rooms. Still others are persons of brooding complexity. In the modern world, where we have had better sources of biography and witness, there has been a whole tradition of startlingly religious figures whose life-styles are not all that attractive. We have valued these people not because of their personality but because they have been able to transcend their personal shortcomings in compelling ways. There is an almost unhealthy tendency to fix with the passion of the amateur psychohistorian on the oddities of a Sören Kierkegaard or the self-abnegation of a Simone Weil. But what makes these people significant is not the queerness of their personalities but what there is about them beyond that queerness. The world, after all, is filled with neurotically motivated persons, yet their quirkiness does not compel us of itself.

The world's religions have recognized the extremes in spirituality and have attempted to deal with extremities by strategies designed to keep saintly asceticism from being an end in itself. Buddhism, for example, is a religion that puts great stock in an ascetic detachment from the false world of materiality. The pursuit of Buddhist detachment is tempered, however, by the equally strong emphasis on Buddhist compassion. Likewise, Christianity preaches "death to self" but sees the death of self within the symbolism of the resurrectional motif of "living in Christ." These large religious paradigms root themselves in the saint's insistence that forgetfulness of self blossoms, ideally, into love of all and love for all.

The seeming eccentricity of the saint must also be seen against the historical and cultural background in which the saint lived. We may find the fierce, almost bizarre, asceticism of the Desert Fathers as a form of fanaticism unless we measure their lives against the late pagan and Neoplatonic appreciation of the ascetic life. The *homines spirituales* presented an ideal form of life for others besides Christian monks. We should remember the impact that the *Life of Saint Anthony* made on Augustine and his friends even before they were baptized Christians. It is a simplism to judge the accidental character of sanctity of a given age by the cultural presuppositions of another age. Karl Rahner has pointed out, wisely, one must say, that just as we speak of a development of doctrine in Christianity, so we must also recognize a development of spirituality.

We must also recognize that however large hearted and generous the saint may be, very few saints seem to be so universal in their appeal as to overcome absolutely the limitations and prejudices of their age. Catholics, for example, might find Kierkegaard's spiritual style too individualistic and too lacking in any liturgical or sacramen-

tal dimension. By contrast, a Protestant might find Saint Thérèse of
Lisieux suffocatingly and cloyingly pious in her writings on spiritual
matters. That is only natural. Kierkegaard became a saint against the
background of (and in reaction to) Danish Lutheranism while Saint
Thérèse was from a bourgeous French family of the late nineteenth
century. In either case, it would be a tragedy to stop at these surface
impressions (which are, for their part, also culturally conditioned) and
miss the true significance of their spiritual or moral message.

This last point bears some closer examination. What distin-
guishes the saint from the merely religious is that the example of their
life is still worthwhile for us now. The example of Saint Thérèse of
Lisieux (1873–1897) is instructive in that regard. Her life was spent
as a cloistered Carmelite nun until her premature death at the age
of twenty-four from tuberculosis. Her fame rests in a short book of
spiritual autobiography, *The Story of a Soul,* published two years after
her death.[10] In style, it is rather like any number of gratefully forgotten pieces of "pious" writing. Its perennial value is to be found in
Thérèse's absolute conviction that one best served God by the willingness to follow what she called the "little way," that is, the doing
of what one could do in a given set of circumstances with the utmost
love of God and purity of intention. She preached the primacy of the
ordinary. When one sees her message unencumbered by the sweet-
ness of her style and the almost coy artlessness of her writing, the
message is basic and true. One is put into a certain place under
certain conditions. The greatest thing that one can give to God is to
do His will here and now with an intense purity of purpose. It was
this message that gripped Mother Teresa of Calcutta. When she
decided to serve the poor, it was Saint Thérèse's "little way" that she
decided to follow. She simply went out into the streets of Calcutta
and began the utterly natural work of serving the needy and destitute.
It was as simple as that. It should also be noted that this decision to
give herself completely to the poor of Calcutta came as a "second
conversion" for Mother Teresa. She had been in India for eighteen
years as a missionary teacher with the Sisters of Loreto. She has said
that on a train on September 10, 1946, she received a "call within
a call." In her own words: "The message was quite clear. I was to

leave the convent and help the poor while living among them. It was an order. I knew where I belonged, but I did not know how to get there."[11] It was that simple "call" that lead Mother Teresa to the streets of Calcutta and from there, to the world.

In my preliminary definition of the saint, I said the religious vision that grips the saint not only changes the person in a radically new way but also *leads others to glimpse the value of that vision.* I now need to specify in greater detail what I mean by that. In brief, my argument is that the saint is a person of heroic sanctity, and the sanctity he or she embodies is a value or a sign-event for others. The basic question is what the saint as sign-event signifies.

It would seem that the life and witness of the saint signifies one of three things: (1) the perennial value of the religious tradition by showing that tradition in a vigorously lived fashion, (2) a model for new ways of living out the religious vision of a given tradition, or (3) a prophetic judgment on those who share the religious tradition but fail to reach up to its claims and/or ideals. Obviously, at times, a number of these elements coalesce. When Saint Francis of Assisi undertook his life of poverty, he showed the Church a new way of understanding the religious life as a mendicant instead of a monk while setting forth a judgment about the wealth and worldliness of the Church of the High Middle Ages.

In the first place, then, the saint is a sign of the vitality of his religious vision. The saint appears at a certain moment and shows the vitality of religious commitment. In such circumstances, the saint becomes what Paul Tillich has called a "sign-event." Every Christian is, in a certain sense, a saint; but when a Christian's love and faith is such that it becomes a sign for others who are grasped by the power and the creativity of that faith or love, then the person is a saint in a more specific and concrete way.

This notion of the person, the saint, as a sign-event is linked to Tillich's notion that revelation is not revelation *in* history but *through* history. History, in turn, is the history of groups as well as personalities. Personalities that reveal through history need not be the grand representatives of history or history's most visible interpreters. They can be simply those personalities who are transparent in their ground of being. Thus, for Tillich, the definition of the saints is, "The persons who are transparent for the Ground of Being which is revealed through them and who are able to enter a revelatory constellation as mediums."[12]

If the saint is a sign-event and a revelation through history, as Tillich would have it, we can legitimately ask what the saint signifies or reveals. The answer, according to Tillich, is that the saint—I use Tillich's terminology here—overcomes the disintegrating forces of personhood in such a way that the saint is a whole person. The radical powers of a person's essence are actualized in an unambiguous way by the "Spiritual Presence." The saint—and this is my terminology —is rooted in the Ground of Being and that Ground is made transparent. Tillich states it eloquently:

> The "saint" (he who is determined by the Spiritual Presence) knows where to go and where not to go. He knows the way between impoverishing asceticism and disrupting libertinism. In the life of most people the question of where to go, in which direction to spread and which direction to make predominant, is a continuous concern. They do not know where to go, and therefore may cease to go at all and permit their life processes to fall into the poverty of anxious self-restriction; others start off in so many directions that they cannot follow up any of them. The Spirit conquers restrictions as well as disruptions by preserving the unity in divergent directions and the unity of the directions which reconverge after they have diverged. They reconverge in the direction of the ultimate.[13]

We might pursue this notion of the saint as a sign-event just a bit further. The saint signifies *something* in concrete circumstances. By using the qualifier "event," I wish to underscore the essentially historical character of the saint's witness. What is it that the saint signifies? One of two things: either the perennial value of the religious vision of life or some new way in which that vision can be incarnated.

First, the saint can give eloquent testimony to the enduring value of certain Christian images or ideals. Our tendency is to think of certain religious values in very abstract terms. We speak of faith, love, poverty, hope, and so on. In a similar fashion, we use certain traditional biblical images such as servant, shepherd, or prophet almost as if they were Platonic archetypes. In the very concrete world of the Gospels, however, these ideals live in specific persons (and, preeminently, in a Person) who exemplify the values. It is the Good Samaritan who exemplifies the meaning of a neighbor, just as the Good Shepherd is the answer to the question, "How much does God love us?"

In the course of Christian history, the saint functions very much like the paradigmatic personages of the Gospels. The saint enfleshes Christian ideals in concrete historical situations and widely divergent historical epochs. Jesus enjoins the life of voluntary poverty "for the Kingdom of God." Saint Benedict, Saint Francis of Assisi, Saint Vincent de Paul, and the hidden saints of the Catholic Worker Movement show us how voluntary poverty should look at given times in our history. All these saints respond to the same value, but they live out their commitment in different ways and according to different modalities. The witness of their lives permits us to see how a value can be lived in a specific and appropriate manner. John Dunne has put the matter nicely with his distinction between the "friends of God" (that is, the saints) and the "common notion":

> We have a choice, if we wish to know God, between learning from the friends of God and learning from the common notion. I would choose to learn from the friends of God. The common notion is a way of interpreting whatever happens, but it does not seem to arise out of any actual communication between God and man. The friends of God, on the contrary, walk and speak with God, experience a love that is "from God and of God and towards God." To actually know God ourselves we will have to enter into the to-and-fro. Maybe from that vantage point we may be able to see the common notion in a new light.[14]

I have said that the saint teaches us the value of the perennial ideals of the Christian vision. In that sense, the saint "relives" the vision of the Gospel. I have emphasized the idea of the continuous vitality of the Christian witness. The other side of that witness, however, is that the saint helps us to understand new and different ways of living out the implications of the Gospel. This new vision not only clarifies the value of the Gospel but it also, at the same time,

judges the inadequacies of the present. In that sense, the witness of
the saint is not merely to show us a new way of being a Christian;
the life of the saint passes a prophetic judgment on our failures "to
bring forth things both old and new." On this characteristic of the
saintly life, Karl Rahner has written,

> They [that is, the saints] are the initiators and the creative models
> of the holiness which happens to be right for, and is the task of, their
> particular age. They create a new style; they prove that a certain form
> of life and activity is a really genuine possibility; they show experimen-
> tally that one can be a Christian even in "this" way; they make a certain
> type of person believable as a Christian type. Their significance begins
> therefore not merely after they are dead. Their death is rather the seal
> put on their task of being creative models, a task which they had in the
> church during their lifetime, and their living on means that the example
> they have given remains in the Church as a permanent form.[15]

Rahner makes one other major point in his discussion of the saints
that bears some scrutiny. He notes that in the lives of the saints, their
style of life or their manifestations of holiness were often not recognized as such by their contemporaries. Indeed, many of the saints
were gravely suspect by the defenders of orthodoxy. The examples are
many: Saint Ignatius Loyola had his share of problems with the
Spanish Inquisition. Saint Robert Bellarmine's theological works
were almost put on the Index (for not being papal enough!). The
works of Saint Thomas Aquinas were proscribed for a time after his
death by the theological faculty of Paris. Saint John of the Cross "did
time" in a monastic prison for his ideas and beliefs. Some saints
managed to live out a style of life while others, who attempted the
same style, found themselves stigmatized as hetereodox. Thus, Saint
Francis of Assisi, with his insistent desire to lead an evangelically pure
life, did not spring up with sudden unexpected singularity. His revolutionary style of Christianity must be seen against the background of
such contemporary movements as the Waldensians, the Poor Men
of Lyon, the Lollards, and other such reform movements in the
medieval Church, which yearned for precisely the same kind of life.
The peculiar genius of Saint Francis was that he carried it off without

finding himself emarginated from the Church in the process.

The point to be emphasized here is that the saints are at the very cutting edge of the Church; they are the harbingers and the prophets of what the Church needs to be and needs to do in a given historical moment. They are the *avant-garde* who testify to the needs of the time. At the same time, they testify to the possibility of sanctity in a given epoch, a sanctity germane to their time and an example that stands historically as an enriching paradigm for the future.

The elements of "past" and "futurity" in the lives of the saints to which I alluded previously may be pursued a bit further. The futurity of the lives of the saints is rooted in an ancient element in the Catholic understanding of the saints. We should remember that the official "certification" of the saints by the process of canonization is founded on the Church's proclamation that the saints are in heaven and, as such, are worthy intercessors. The fact that the saints are in heaven is the crucial point. Aside from their efforts of intercession, the saints are eschatological signs, that is, they point to the hope that every Christian has—the hope to be in heaven with the entire company of the Blessed. It is for this reason that the Fathers of the Second Vatican Council treated the subject of the saints in the seventh chapter of the *Dogmatic Constitution of the Church (Lumen Gentium),* a chapter that deals with the "eschatological nature" of the Pilgrim Church. The council briefly affirmed the exemplary function of the saints but then went on to add that by sensing our communion with those who already stand before God, "we are responding to the deepest vocation of the church and partaking in a foretaste of the liturgy of consummate glory" (*Lumen Gentium* VII, 51).[16] This eschatological element is stated just as explicitly in the Council's *Constitution on the Liturgy,* where the liturgy as a foretaste of the heavenly liturgy is described as singing a "hymn to the Lord's glory with all the warriors of the heavenly army; venerating the memory of the saints, *we hope for some part and fellowship with them*" (*Sacrosanctum Concilium* I, 8; emphasis added).

Yet the futurity of the saints need not be understood only in this strict eschatological sense. Futurity is also a part of the exemplary function of the saints, as Karl Rahner's understanding of the saints

rather obliquely suggested. At certain points in the Church's experience, there needs to be (or better, there seems to appear) persons who
"break" with the current understanding of how the faith is to be
incarnated in actual practice for the future. Actual modes of doing
things do not seem to be sufficient for the cultural conditions in
which the Church finds herself. People then emerge, often in the face
of tremendous hostility or misunderstanding, and point to a "new
way." The history of the Church is full of examples of such persons.
There is nothing in our current experience that should lead us to
think it should be different in our own era.

The current rise of feminist consciousness in Christianity provides one good illustration of what is being suggested here. Feminist
awareness did not start in the Church; it started in the larger culture,
and with some difficulty, impinged on the consciousness of the
Church. Today, feminism in the Church makes itself felt both by a
heightened awareness of the ways women have been denigrated in
the tradition as well as specific demands for redress from various
forms of oppressive behavior in the Church. The most pressing (and
highly charged) contemporary demand is for women priests. Such a
demand reflects the feminine desire to participate equally in the
liturgico-sacramental power and ministry. The demand for women
priests, an eradication of sexism, a better understanding of patriarch-
ical structures that have burdened the tradition, and such are not
discrete demands. They are signs of a change in consciousness, a
change Beatrice Bruteau has called the "next revolution in consciousness," that is, the first signs of a new age that will be a "revolution
in the sense of being a new 'turn' in this mounting spiral of fluctuat-
ing but evolving consciousness."[17]

This revolution in consciousness does not happen by some inexorable law in the very nature of things. Consciousness is raised and
made possible by persons; any evolutionary advance made in our
consciousness now will be made by the exercise of our own freedom.
Put another way, feminist consciousness will happen when women
(and, *mutatis mutandis,* men) show forth new ways of being Christian that well up from the free and voluntary expression of their own
consciousness of being Christians in a new way. When the late Pope

Paul VI said that women could not be priests because they were not images of Jesus, he was speaking from the position of "old consciousness," a consciousness that was as culture bound as that of the pope who balked at the idea of the early Jesuits not reciting the Divine Office in common because it had never been done that way before in religious life.

When such conspicuous women appear (they may well have already appeared) in the Church, they will exemplify what it means to be a Christian in a consciously new way. At the appearance of such saints (for that is what a saint is), they will reveal the past/future dimension of which I have spoken. By their life, they will show that the Christian tradition has come to a new understanding; and in that recognition, they will become a standard against which others in the future will be judged. In short, their lived-out consciousness will be the instrument for teaching others.

It is precisely because the saint is one who in his or her life shows the deep possibilities of what it means to be truly religious that we call a saint "holy" (compare the Hebrew *kdsh*, set apart)—one who is "separated" or "set apart" by the presence of the Divine. The saint sets forth the meaning of God in the living out of her life. True hagiography should be an ideal locus for what Sallie TeSelle calls "intermediate theology," that is, seeing in the lives of another not merely a consistency with certain doctrinal formulations, but a resonance and a depth that reflects back on the reader or observer of that life in such a way as to illuminate or clarify.[18] In that sense, the life of the saint should act like a parable: It should shock us into a heightened and new sense of God's presence (and judgment) in our own life.

The life of the saint is, in the root sense of that term, a transcendent one. Transcendence *(trans-scendere)* literally means to "go up and over." Every religious life story is transcendent in the sense that a person assents to new elements in life and then goes (or grows) beyond them. These life elements are not necessarily extraordinary —they are, in fact, the basics of being: world, people, sexuality, death. But they summon the religious person to deep and creative engagement with those events, realities, and relationships.[19] The person who goes up to and beyond those events, realities, and relationships in such a luminous way as to be a pointer for others to the path of transcendence is the true saint of faith.

It should be obvious that such an understanding of the saint is a modest one when compared to those who are enrolled officially in the calendar of the Church. My definition of the saint includes those who might come into our lives in very undramatic and limited ways. Ideally, those persons who are canonized by the Church have characteristics worthy of universal emulation. In practice, however, this is not often the case. Saints often are canonized because they meet the demanding criteria of a specific process. This doesn't lessen their holiness, but it may say little about their paradigmatic value. Early in his pontificate (December 1978), Pope John Paul II approved three persons for beatification, the penultimate step before canonization. The three included a nineteenth-century priest (the Salesian priest, Father August Czartoryski, who died in 1893) and two nuns who died in this century: Sister Francesca Aviat of France (died 1914) and Sister Giuseppina Bakhita of the Sudan, who died in 1947. With all respect to the merit of these servants of God, one could hardly describe them as recognized models for the entire Christian church.

Our understanding of the saint would dwell more on those persons who lived lives that were not only set apart (holy) because of their luminous spirituality but were also lives that served as genuine catalysts for the religious lives of others. Their lives, despite aberrations, deficiencies, and eccentricities, would be such that others could find ways of incarnating their values into their own lives. In that sense, the saint is a charism in the Pauline sense of being given for the general good (1 Cor. 12:7) of the whole body of the faithful. Every Christian is called to be a saint *(hagios)* in the biblical sense of that term. Some people are given the gift of responding to God's grace in such a way that their gift builds up the Christian community.

If we think of the saint as a charism, we can also appreciate that the saint might be in some kind of dialectical tension with the structured Church. This kind of tension has always existed in the Church. Yet the tension is not an unhealthy one; in the last analysis, to fail to recognize genuine charismata in the Church (and that would include the charism of conspicuous sanctity) "casts a shadow on the title deed of the church [which] leads to conformism and inhabits all dynamism."[20] The criterion, then, for the recognition of the saint cannot merely be some institutional process. There must be room in the Church for the acknowledgment of those saints who would not fit into comfortable categories. The de facto situation is that many faithful Christians recognize saints who are not (and probably never will be) in the calendar. That is not merely a manifestation of "popular" religion; it is an empirical indication that heroic sanctity is as much a charism as it is an office in the Christian community.

It is not the purpose of this discussion to make invidious comparisons between those who are canonized as saints and those who are not canonized but who may be considered by a large number of people as equally worthy of canonization. It is my purpose to suggest that if we are interested in lives of others who might nourish and enrich our own religious life, we might well look beyond the canon of the saints as it is officially proposed for our veneration. One index of these "unofficial" saints would be their demonstrated capacity to inspire those who might otherwise be indifferent to the claims of Christianity. By that criterion, to cite some random examples, a Count Leo Tolstoy, with all of his eccentricities and his narrowness, is a saint. His later life was marked by an appropriation of a deep Christianity rooted in a sustained reflection on the Beatitudes of Jesus. His "living out" of that Gospel vision (truncated though it may have been) was persuasive enough to inspire, among others, a Gandhi. Gandhi was able to transform the Tolstoyan vision into a radical new understanding that, in turn, returned to the West and was acted out in the nonviolence of a Martin Luther King, Jr. In a similar manner, a Thomas Merton (whose life, one suspects, would give the *Promotor Fidei* some ammunition) brought to the fore certain insights of the monastic and contemplative life in such a way as to shape the lives of a large number of persons, not all of whom were in the bosom of the Church. Other persons—with varying degrees of doctrinal orthodoxy—have had a similar impact on the religious imagination of our time. One thinks of Albert Schweitzer, Pope John XXIII, Peter Maurin, and Simone Weil.

It goes without saying that there are a large number of such persons who will never come to the public eye but who function in the same way for more restricted groups of people. On occasion, the Church itself has raised to the altars humble people who took modest tasks or lived simple lives with luminous spirituality. What characterizes these people is the fidelity and the creativity of their lives in the age and culture in which they live.

To say that the saint is an exemplar or a paradigm is not to say that the saint is automatically lovable as a person or that his particular spiritual emphasis can be completely emulated. In fact, quite the contrary is often true. Most of the saints seem to be more admitted than fully emulated. Most people would not like to end up at the stake like Saint Joan of Arc or lead the ascetic life of Saint Bernard of Clairvaux. It was the "seriousness" of their life, however, that gave them the moral and spiritual credibility to correct the temporal and spiritual powers of their time. If the saints cannot be fully emulated, their witness cannot be ignored. It is the intensity and seriousness of their lives that compels attention.

The value of the saintly personality, eccentricities and all, is that it provides us a norm or standard by which we may measure our religious seriousness. As William James observed, despite the Beatitudes in the Gospel, the teachings of Tolstoy, or the example of the Quakers, most people believe in fighting fire with fire. Yet the exemplary value of the "extravagances of human tenderness" of a Leo Tolstoy demonstrates alternative ways of behavior. Such persons who do not live according to the conventional norm act out the potentialities of human goodness through the example of their own self-transcendence: "They are impregnators of the world, vivifiers and animators of potentialities of goodness which but for them would live forever dormant. It is not possible to be quite as mean as we naturally are, when they have passed before us."[21]

Beyond the valuable example that the saint gives to the individual, there is the equally powerful value of the saint as one who points to a better social order or who stands in criticism of the actual deficiences in the present order of things. In that sense, certain saints project fantasies about a "better" relationship among all persons or protest the "unsaintly" conditions of the many. As James notes, Utopian social thinkers and saints have analogous functions: "They help to break the edge of the general reign of hardness and are slow leavens of a better order."[22] James's point with respect to the saints is not unlike Harvey Cox's observation that such movements as monasticism were (and, to an extent, remain) experiments in political fantasy in which the world is shown an "as it might be" world of ordered Christian charity and fraternity.[23] Such experiments might not change the world, but they provide other scenarios and alternatives. They testify to the high potentialities for humanization at the social level.

I have argued in this chapter that the saint is a person whose life is so centered on a profound religious vision that it is radically different. That difference is so apparent to others for its quality and depth that the sympathetic observer can see the value of the religious vision that has grasped the saint. In seeing that value, the person who encounters the saint can begin to understand the perennial value of the religious tradition that informs the life of the saint or glimpse new ways in which a religious life can be lived out. The perception of the value of the saint's life also carries, implicitly or explicitly, a judgment on the way an observer lives. The saint, in short, serves both a paradigmatic and prophetic function.

In 1848, John Henry Newman was involved with Father Frederick Faber in a publishing venture to issue a series of lives of the saints. The volumes, to be translated from the Italian, were baroque hagiographies, rich in the miraculous and the strange but short on historical plausibility. The series eventually failed amid a swirl of misunderstanding and controversy. A preface, never published with the books that did appear, has been preserved among Newman's papers. It is a splendid description of the role of saints in Christian life and, for our purposes, an apt summary of the basic argument of this chapter:

> They [that is, the saints] are the popular evidence of Christianity, and the most complete and logical evidence while the most popular. It

requires time, learning, the power of attention and logical consecutive-
ness and comprehensiveness, to survey the church in all ages and places
as one, and to recognize it (as to the intellect, it is, and must be distinctly
recognized) as the work of God alone; to most of us it is the separate,
and in one sense incomplete, portions of this great phenomenon which
turn one's mind to Catholicism; but in the life of a saint, we have a
microcosm, or the whole work of God, a perfect work from beginning
to end, yet one which may be bound between two boards, and mastered
by the most unlearned. The exhibition of a person, his thoughts, his
words, his acts, his trials, his features, his beginnings, his growth, his end,
have a charm to everyone; and where he is a saint they have a divine
influence and persuasion, a power of exercising and eliciting the latent
elements of divine grace in individual readers as no other reading can
have.[24]

NOTES

1. Karl Rahner, "The Church of the Saints." In *Theological Investigations*, vol.
    3 (Baltimore: Helicon Press, 1967), pp. 91–105. This chapter is also indebted
    to a reading of Romano Guardini, *The Saints in Daily Christian Life* (Philadel-
    phia: Chilton Books, 1966) and Rene Latourelle, "La Sainteté signe de la
    Révélation." In *Gregorianum*, vol. 46 (1965), pp. 36–65.
2. M. Nicolau et al., *Sacrae Theologiae Summa*, 4 vols. (Madrid: BAC, 1955).
3. Paul Tillich, *Systematic Theology*, vol. 1 (Chicago: University of Chicago Press,
    1967), p. 122.
4. Dolores Brien, "The Catholic Revival Revisited," *Commonweal* (December
    21, 1979), p. 716.
5. William James, *The Varieties of Religious Experience* (New York: Mentor
    Books of the New American Library, 1958), p. 212. All citations are from this
    edition.
6. James, *Varieties*, pp. 216–217. Latourelle, "La Sainteté," p. 57, cites the follow-
    ing characteristics of sanctity: (1) a value that encourages others to participate
    by imitation, (2) a profound harmony between the ideal of the Gospel and the
    life of the saint, and (3) a complex intensity of life corresponding to the
    intensity of the Gospel itself.
7. James, *Varieties*, p. 218.
8. Ibid.
9. Ibid., p. 282.
10. There are many editions of this work; the most reliable and scholarly is Saint
    Thérèse, *Story of a Soul*, trans. John Clarke, OCD (Washington: Institute of

Carmelite Studies, 1975). See also the recent *St. Therese of Lisieux: Her Last Conversations*, ed. and trans. John Clarke, OCD (Washington: Institute of Carmelite Studies, 1977). On the influence of the "little way" of Saint Thérèse on Mother Teresa of Calcutta, see Michael T. Kaufman, "The World of Mother Teresa," *New York Times Magazine* (December 9, 1979), p. 42.

11. Quoted in Kaufman, "The World of Mother Teresa," p. 98.

12. Tillich, *Systematic Theology*, vol. 1, p. 121.

13. Ibid., vol. 3, p. 270.

14. John S. Dunne, *The Reasons of the Heart: A Journey into Solitude and Back Again into the Human Circle* (Notre Dame: University of Notre Dame Press, 1978), p. 2.

15. *Theological Investigations*, vol. 3, p. 100.

16. All quotes from the conciliar documents of the Second Vatican Council are from Walter Abbott and Joseph Gallagher, eds., *The Documents of Vatican II* (New York: Guild Press, 1966).

17. Beatrice Bruteau, "Neo Feminism and the Next Revolution in Consciousness," *Cross Currents* (Summer 1977), p. 171. This fine essay first appeared in *Anima* (Spring 1977), pp. 170–182. On the rise of feminist consciousness in this country, I have been helped by Gayle Graham Yates, *What Women Want: The Ideas of the Movement* (Cambridge: Harvard University Press, 1975).

18. Compare her important work on story and theology: Sallie TeSelle, *Speaking in Parables* (Philadelphia: Fortress Press, 1975).

19. These ideas are largely indebted to Joseph Powers, SJ, "The Art of Believing," *Theological Studies* (December 1978), p. 667.

20. Estevao Bettencourt, "Charism." In *Sacramentum Mundi*, ed.Karl Rahne *et al.*, vol. 1 (New York: Herder and Herder, 1968), p. 284.

21. James, *Varieties*, p. 277.

22. Ibid., p. 279.

23. Harvey Cox, *The Feast of Fools* (Cambridge: Harvard University Press, 1969), p. 82.

24. The entire fragment can be found in Vincent Ferrer Blehl, SJ, ed., *The Essential Newman* (New York: Mentor Omega Books, 1963), pp. 235–236.

CHAPTER 4

The Hidden Dimensions of Modern Sanctity

IN MY previous discussion of the notion of sainthood, I noted that the saint sets forth religious values that are both perennial and new. I further insisted that the newness of a saint's witness shows a given age that sanctity is possible even in this or that set of peculiar cultural circumstances. The saint, as it were, rises up in history and responds to, or reacts against, the characteristics of the historical moment.

We can now legitimately ask whether there is a sanctity unique to our own modern world. In general terms, it seems obvious that the "style" of sanctity differs according to historical epochs and peculiar situations. After all, the piety of Saint Augustine is a far cry from that of Saint Bernard of Clairvaux, just as the character of Charismatic piety differs widely from that found in a Carthusian hermitage today. In another sense, there is a certain timelessness to piety and spirituality. To read a volume of Thomas Merton is to recognize that his writings echo a long tradition of spiritual writing. To say that a Thomas Merton speaks to the modern world is not to say that he is free from the influence of his spiritual ancestors.

In our own time, there have been saintly personalities whose piety seems to be completely free from modern influences. In that sense, as we shall see in some depth later in this work, the saintly vocation is timeless. Let it suffice for now to observe that the life of the Italian stigmatic Padre Pio would have been much the same had he lived one hundred or even five hundred years ago. His piety, discipline, asceticism, alleged thaumaturgic powers, charity, and pastoral zeal—all of those manifestations of the life he led that marked him as conspicuously holy—are relatively timeless. His life transcended the particular historical exigencies of his milieu. That jets flew over his convent or that his mountain village bristled with television antennas or that the young of that village fled the mountains for the large industrial centers of postwar Italy had no effect on his daily rounds as a Capuchin friar.

It should be clear, however, that this ahistorical style of life does not sum up everything that can be said about spirituality in our age. Indeed, if there is a criticism to be made about much of the conventional view of holiness (at least in official Catholic circles), it is that this somewhat ahistorical view has been seen as normative. It is too easily assumed by some that heroic sanctity worthy to be called sainthood is coterminous with ecclesial regularity. While it would be audacious to affirm that true sanctity and ecclesial fidelity are mutually exclusive, it is not immediately apparent that they are necessarily in tandem.

Whatever else secularization may mean—and the concept is fraught with difficulty—it does certainly mean this: The power and persuasion of institutional religion does not command the unquestioned assent it once did. The church(es) do not bear the same weight in the world as do those large institutions that shape Western culture. The parish or convent or retreat house or mission station does not compete either in prestige or impact with the other massive institutions of modern civilization.

It is almost a commonplace to assert that our culture is different from that of past ages and requires different strategies for setting forth the spiritual vision of the Gospel. As a natural consequence of this situation, the styles of life that incarnate that vision are also going to be different. But in what way?

It is difficult to generalize an answer to that question, but one thing does seem clear: Many of the persons who have been considered "modern saints" lived hidden lives. That is not to deny that

certain persons of outstanding spiritual character received the approbation of worldwide attention. For years, Albert Schweitzer stood as
a model for ethical Christianity. There was something compelling
about a man with enormous intellectual and artistic gifts who would
devote himself to the succor of suffering people far from the cultural
and national center of his own people. Mother Teresa of Calcutta was
recognized by the world in the form of a Nobel Peace Prize. I could
multiply examples of this kind. They illustrate that modern culture
is not impervious to the attractions of goodness or holiness.

The hiddenness of modern sanctity derives from the fact that
large parts of twentieth-century culture are either indifferent or positively hostile to religious values. The active life of Pastor Dietrich
Bonhoeffer, for example, was an exemplary one. He was a political
activist, a concerned pastor, and a fertile Christian theologian and
thinker. It was, however, in the crucible of a Gestapo prison cell that
his person changed from heroism to sanctity. Bonhoeffer has been
important for subsequent generations of Christians because he was
able to maintain and nourish his deep faith in an essentially dehumanizing and alien environment. The posthumous publication of his
Letters and Papers from Prison permitted us to see a person who was
not merely heroic but saintly. It was only because those papers were
saved that we could glimpse a spiritual life that would have meaning
for us being developed. The hidden witness of his religious fidelity
became apparent almost fortuitously.

The revelation of Bonhoeffer's hidden life is not an exception in
our day. His life was lived, of course, in the most extreme of circumstances. Other figures have illustrated their passionate involvement
with God in less extreme, but very typically modern ways. Who
would have thought that Dag Hammarskjöld, a man of action in the
world, an urbane intellectual, and, at his death in 1961, the secretary
general of the United Nations, would have been, in the most private
of manner, a passionately religious person of almost mystical intensity? Hammarskjöld never felt free to express his deep spirituality by
overt acts of church allegiance. He felt that such activities would have
prejudiced his position with many of his United Nation colleagues.
That fact, in itself, tells us something about the way certain styles of

religious heroism must be worked out in our time. Hammarskjöld's life reflected a precarious balance between the demands placed on him as an international diplomat and his own profoundly mystical temperament. He learned to bridge those two worlds and to reconcile, at least partially, the old tension between the *vita activa* and the *vita contemplativa*. He demonstrated in his life the truth of an observation that he himself had once made: "In our era the road to holiness necessarily passes through the world of action."[1]

It would be hard to think of two persons more different biographically and temperamentally than Dietrich Bonhoeffer and Dag Hammarskjöld. Yet, even in their polar differences, they reflect something not atypical of our time: the search for holiness in situations not supportive of their aspirations. A comparison of these two men is not meant to suggest they are "typical" saints; in fact, they may represent certain extremes within which the antagonism of holiness and culture is not so glaring. Yet, for all that, the saintly life as it develops in the most hostile of environments is of some interest to us. Holiness in such conditions more clearly reflects the unquenchable nature of the desire for God. Our recent history has provided us with many laboratories to test the truth of sanctity in such hostile situations.

While the twentieth century, which opened with the discoveries of Einstein and Freud, has made magnificent contributions to human culture and scientific advances, it has also been a century of unparalleled violence and human dislocation. Modern violence arose not only because of advances in the technology of violence and warfare, but also through the emergence of totalitarian systems that, in the name of ideology, slaughtered millions of citizens. Richard L. Rubenstein has argued that such mass killing, unprecedented in recorded history, can only be understood against the social background of a secularized and bureaucratically organized society where the older moral constraints of Western culture are eroded or entirely gone.[2]

In the worst totalitarian systems of the century—one thinks immediately of Stalinist Russia or Nazi Germany—it was axiomatic that the prevailing system keep complete social control over its citizens. Deviance was unthinkable and suspected deviants were, in the lugubrious vocabulary so common to our modern ears, "purged," "re-educated," "deported," "resettled," or, in the case of deviant peoples, subject to a "final solution." While wholesale wars have been fought to overcome the most aggressive of these systems, others are accepted as a necessary result of a *Realpolitik*. In more recent times, there have been attempts within totalitarian cultures themselves for a few brave individuals to speak out, whether singly or as parts of small groups, against the worst aspects of totalitarian society. The justly praised "dissidents" of the Eastern Bloc nations and the human rights voices of Latin American dictatorships have all been effective counterbalances to the absolutist pretensions of these total societies. If Eurocommunists now regard the Soviet Union as an "antimodel" or Jean Paul Sartre could protest a French visit of a Soviet official (a generation ago Sartre asked for a cessation of criticism of Stalinist methods so as not to scandalize the French proletariat!), a large measure of gratitude must be given to the moral impact of Aleksandr Solzhenitsyn's revelations of the Gulag.[3]

The "nay saying" of the protesting individual who refuses the totalitarian ideology as antihuman represents one of the bright moral forces in a century not conspicuous for its morality. The very presence of such individuals among us has been a sign that the human spirit still thirsts for a transcendental affirmation of the worth of the individual and the right of the individual to live with a modicum of personal dignity and in some communal bond with others. Such persons are not merely heroic (although it has required eximious bravery to be a protester), but saintly, that is, they act as models by being set apart in their thirst for the true and the good; and this thirst derives from a deep sense that such rights are grounded ontologically in the very nature of being in the world. Beyond that, these saintly protesters are willing to give all to testify to that right.

We do not ordinarily think of such persons under the rubric of saints. It would be somewhat facile to make such a claim and still maintain any precise notion of the saint. What is clear, however, is that there is a tradition that, in fact, does link the notion of heroic resistance to totalitarianism or militant atheism and sanctity. The analogy of the human struggle for personal dignity and heroic sanctity does not derive from putting labels on such persons. The analogy arises from the intense scrutiny that sensitive persons have made of the nature of humanity in its struggle against the countervailing forces of dehumanization. What analogy suffices, these persons ask, to explain the struggle for goodness, self-affirmation, and love for others in a world implacably hostile to these aspirations? One answer has been that it takes a saint to survive such conditions or to transform them into something else.

The literary roots of this idea go back to the great Russian novelists of the last century, Leo Tolstoy and Fyodor Dostoevsky. Both men were bedeviled by the cultural and religious crises of their times. Tolstoy turned in his mature years to a radically simplified form of Christianity based on the Sermon on the Mount. His last great novel, *Resurrection,* was an attempt to characterize how this simple form of Christian anarchy could be carried out in life. Prince Nekhludov, the hero of the novel, undergoes a long series of conversions in which he sloughs off his wealth, position, and egotism to be left in the end with an unshakable conviction about the centrality of the Gospels for his life. A measure of this conversionary process was his willingness to live as a voluntary exile in Siberia with a woman he once wronged.

Tolstoy's saint was a judgment on the corruption, hypocrisy, and hollowness of both church and state in prerevolutionary Russia. Dostoevsky was not unaware of these failings, but his concern was a wider and more philosophical one. He, perhaps more than any other figure in the last century, was concerned with the implications of systematic atheism. "If God does not exist then everything is possible," says one of his characters. As a remedy for the anarchy and violence he saw as implicit in atheism, Dostoevsky proposed, as a counterforce, a powerful faith in the reality of God and the compassionate power of Christ. This countervailing faith shaped the character of Father Zosima and Aloysha in *The Brothers Karamazov* as well as the mystical Prince Myshkin in *The Idiot.*

The Russian literary tradition of the fictional saint sprang from the deep Christian faith of the authors themselves. What seems to be new about the fiction of our century, at least that fiction written in response to modern totalitarianism, is that certain modern authors have attempted to spell out explicitly a theory of sanctity somewhat removed from the orthodox standards of Christianity. The starting point of some of this fiction was an intense interest in Christ-like figures who live and move in totalitarian settings. Much of this fiction is less religious in the conventional sense of the term, although one still hears echos and reverberations of the older hieratic language of traditional Christianity. R. W. B. Lewis's *The Picaresque Saint* was a classic attempt to see these marginal fictional heroes under the rubric of sanctity. His usage of the term "saint" was not merely rhetorical. It was a deliberate strategy to study the conditions of sanctity in a world where explicit religiousness is hard to come by. For Lewis, and any number of other commentators on the fiction of the first half of this century, the hidden saints of the modern secularized world were those marginal outsiders whose struggles for personal and social integrity were saintly in the sense that they strove mightily for the real in a world that was rapidly becoming a violent sham.

In the late 1930s and early 1940s, there were a number of novels that took up this theme as a central concern. Theodore Ziolkowski has shown that the heroes of these novels (Jim Casy in *Grapes of Wrath*, Rubashov in *Darkness at Noon*, the unnamed priest in *The Power and the Glory*, and Pietro Spina in *Bread and Wine*) were transformed Jesus figures.[4] They fit under a rubric Ziolkowski has called the "Comrade Jesus" figure. In other words, these fictional heroes reflected the holiness, self-sacrifice, and giving to others in a "new way." They stood in a figural relationship to the paradigmatic figure of self-giving: Jesus Christ. For this period of history, according to these novelists, the presence of Jesus was to be conceptualized in a new revelatory fashion. Jesus was to be found incarnated anew in out-of-the-way, hidden places. It should also be noted, as Ziolkowski has argued, that these fictional characters are not figures in a "what if Jesus came again" novel; they are persons in their own setting who manifest in their lives echoes of the deeds, values, and transformative actions of Jesus.

It is not inappropriate to turn to the novel for an understanding of the hidden dimension of sanctity in our time. A good deal of hagiography, after all, is fictional. From the fertile imaginings of the medieval writer, we have received the compassionate figure of a Saint

Veronica, who spurned the crowd to perform an act of mercy, or a Saint George, who became a charged symbol of self-giving and chivalric heroism. In fact, contrary to the conventional wisdom, one could argue that the very fictional nature of a good deal of hagiography presents not an insuperable difficulty but a fecund opportunity for the modern religious person. It helps us to understand one way of reading the imaginative literature of our time. Literature, after all, not only carries along our most cherished myths from the past but also throws up new, and often inchoate, possibilities of what we would like to be or what we ought to be.

Perhaps no writer in this century has written as compellingly about the need for a new sanctity in our world as has the Italian novelist Ignazio Silone (penname for Secondo Tranquilli, who died in 1978). Silone was the quintessential outsider. He had been a founding member of the Italian Communist party but in the 1920s left it in disgust with the repressively mendacious policies of Stalin and the Comintern. He was profoundly Christian but remained outside the confines of the Catholic Church all of his life. Because of his vigorous anti-Fascism, he had to leave Italy in 1930 for a sustained exile in Davos, Switzerland. His first novels were published in Switzerland in German, and it was not until the end of the war that his native Italy even had a chance to read his work. His return to Italy did little to elevate his status in his native country. The Marxist critics could not forget his departure from the party; the Catholics were nervous about his doctrinal orthodoxy; the formalists had little taste for his rough, unadorned prose. Above all, the Italians could not understand how Silone could be so popular outside his own country. Until he achieved the status of a literary elder statesman in the last decade of his life, Silone was an enigma in Italy.

Part of the enigma of Silone is to be found in his conviction that it is the individual who is the ultimate locus of moral authority and that a person as moral authority has a deep obligation to resist encrusted power, whether that power emanates from party, church, or nation. Silone seemed to be in direct opposition to the communal sympathies of the Italian *ethos* that puts such an emphasis on the communal bonds of social existence. Silone recognized that in perilous times, it is the individual who must act out of a deep sense of personal obligation, worth, and passion. In his most famous novel, *Bread and Wine*, Silone stated that conviction most eloquently. It was also the novel where he explicated his notion that such an individual could be considered a new kind of saint.

Early in the novel, the old anti-Fascist priest Don Benedetto dug out a composition once written by his former student, Pietro Spina (the hero of the novel) to read it to a group of Spina's former classmates. The theme of that composition is also the theme of the novel. It is the statement of a desire for a new kind of sanctity: "If it would not be such a bore after one's death to be placed over an altar and adored and prayed to by a bunch of unknown people, mainly old women, I would like to be a saint. I don't want to live according to sheer circumstance and material comfort but, without caring about the consequences, I would like to live every moment of my life struggling for that which seems to me right and just."[5]

That Pietro Spina lived such a life and was, as a consequence, a new kind of saint is the burden of Silone's novel. That this was a new kind of sanctity is clear from the contrast between Pietro and a young girl he meets, Christina. Christina represents the old sanctity; she is convinced that the best way to serve God is by the traditional ascesis of leaving the world to serve, in silence and prayer, with total and dedicated abnegation. She had decided to become a nun and her convictions about the radical dichotomy between the world and God are absolute. Christina's simple faith forced Pietro to reexamine his own rigidity and caused him to soften his attitude from ideology to compassion. Christina caused him to move from the abstract idea of class to the real level of persons. Yet Pietro could not do this by changing into the old pattern of Catholic asceticism. He undergoes a conversion through the example of Christina, but it is not a conversion to Christian's style of life. Silone's judgment of the inadequacy of her spirituality in modern times is summed up in the highly charged ending that Christina meets as the novel reaches its conclusion: Pietro and Christina are fleeing through a mountain pass in a snowstorm. Christina falters and wolves close in on her as she loses her way in the storm.

How is the "new" sanctity articulated for Silone? The answer is clear and simple: In times of extreme social and political distress, God is hidden; and it is the saint who makes God reappear. This new epiphany of God may come in strange and unexpected ways as the old devices for Divine self-disclosure are replaced by new ones. It is central to *Bread and Wine* that the hero live his clandestine life disguised as a priest. There is little doubt that for the author, Pietro is a new kind of priest living under the guise of the old. In the climactic scene of the novel (from which the novel gets its title) Pietro and some poor peasants share the rude country meal of bread and wine. This meal is a hidden Eucharist now being celebrated by a new kind of priest and in a new "church." In a scene charged with biblical and patristic allusions, the hero of the novel shares bread and wine with the peasant family, remarking that "the bread is made from many ears of corn . . . therefore it signifies unity. The wine is made from many grapes, and therefore it, too, signifies unity. A unity of similar things, equal and united. Therefore it means truth and brotherhood too; these are things that go well together."[6] Should anyone object that such a sentiment is merely a sentimentalizing of socialist doctrine, it would do well to remember some words from the oldest Eucharistic prayer we possess outside of the New Testament: "As this broken bread was scattered over the hills and, then, when gathered, became one mass, so may thy Church be gathered from the ends of the earth into they kingdom. For thine is the power and the glory through Jesus Christ for evermore" *(The Didache)*.

The "bread and wine" scene in Silone's novel is not a parody of orthodox Eucharistic theology; it is an attempt to state the essential notion of Eucharist as communion—*cum unione*—union with another. It attempts to flesh out the primordial idea of a sacred meal: Shared eating creates companionship (compare "companion," from the Latin *cum pane*, that is, a "bread sharer") and brotherhood ("brother," possibly from the old German *brod*, bread).

It would be false to think that Silone is trying to change "supernatural" religion into some kind of "humanism" or "natural" religion. Silone has always believed that parallel to the "official" story of the Church in Italy and its theology, there was another history and another theology. This "underground church" was rooted in the apocalyptic utopianism nourished throughout the Middle Ages by the visionary claims of the Calabrian mystic, Joachim of Flora. Joachim envisioned a "Third Age," the Age of the Spirit, in which all the institutions of the "Second Age" (the Age of the Son)—the Church, the temporal kingdoms of the world—would be judged and brought down, thus ushering in an egalitarian utopia based on the principle of love and the mutual bonding of all persons in the Spirit. That Third Age does not arrive; it is always in the process of arriving.

In the introduction of his 1968 play, *L'avventura di un povero cristiano (The Adventures of a Humble Christian)*, Silone called this alternative stream of Christianity a *contropartita*, which, in context, means something like the "loyal opposition." The play itself is an illustration of that idea. The central character of the play is the hermit turned Pope Celestine V, who, after a few months on the papal throne, resigned his office and returned to the mountains of Abbruzi to resume his life as a hermit. For Dante, Celestine represented a weakness that was neither good enough for heaven nor bad enough for hell; accordingly, Dante stigmatized him as the one who made the "great refusal" (*gran rifiuto;* see *Inferno*, III) and, by his cowardice, paved the way for Dante's hated enemy, Boniface VIII, to become pope. For Silone, on the other hand, Celestine was a hero and a saint because Celestine saw the power of the papacy, experienced it, and found the grace to turn his back on it. For Silone, Celestine was a "countersign" to the power pretensions of the Church and a pure sign of radical fidelity to the spirit of the Gospel in its hiddenness and poverty.

For Silone, then, true sanctity is rooted in a radical grasp of the Gospel and an affirmation of that Gospel by personal witness in opposition to structures and powers. In all of Silone's novels, it is the individual who is first seized by this moral imperative and reflects this basic attitude. In his first novel, *Fontamara* (1933), it is the "solitary stranger" *(solito sconsciuto)* who teaches the oppressed peasants to affirm themselves as persons; in *Bread and Wine*, Pietro Spina is the catalyst for the others whose lives impinge on his own and, in that contact, find encouragement; in *The Adventures of a Humble Chris-*

tian, it is the simple refusal of Celestine that emergizes the mystical movement of reform.

This emphasis on the need for radical appropriation of the Gospel on the part of the individual should not lead one to suppose that Silone privatized religion. He felt that when an individual confronted the Gospel in a serious and total way, a new germ was there ready to breed community anew. The sequel to *Bread and Wine*, pointedly enough, was entitled *The Seed Beneath the Snow* (1941). The conversion of Pietro would be completed after the manner of the Gospel: "So is the kingdom of God as if a man should cast seed into the earth" (Matt. 4:26). The central metaphor of that novel is to be found in the close relationship between Pietro and a deaf-mute, Infante. Pietro created friendship and communion against almost impossible odds. He was not only able to communicate with Infante, but learned to love this wounded person in such a way that he was able to offer his own life for him; it is the ultimate act in the imitation of Christ.

The "hiddenness" of Christ, only partially revealed in the lives of a few individuals, is reminiscent of Pascal's observation that Jesus will be on the cross until the end of the world. For Silone, there are moments when the promise of God becomes transparent as this or that person shows the validity and the liveliness of that promise. These are eruptions of Christ in a time of waiting. In this tension-filled period before the Eschaton, a hidden saint may encourage us not to despair of the future promise. In a stage version of *Bread and Wine* (titled, significantly enough, *And He Hid Himself*), Silone made this point forcefully in the introduction to the play: "In the Sacred History of man on earth, it is still Good Friday. Men who 'hunger and thirst after righteousness' are still derided, persecuted, and put to death. The spirit of man is still forced to save himself in hiding."[7] As if to reinforce this point, in the play, a heterodox friar, Fra Giochino (a reference, undoubtedly, to Joachim of Flora) tells a despairing girl: "I say to you that He is still here on earth; in hiding, certainly, and in agony, but on this earth still. As long as He is not dead, we mustn't despair. And perhaps it is for us to see that he is not allowed to die."[8]

The point being urged here is that for Silone, no mere armchair observer of totalitarian societies, our times will demand a sanctity that is not always obvious, a sanctity that is epiphanic, hidden, and only discovered by those who will look beyond the obvious facades of power politics or the predominant culture.

Silone is less esteemed today as a writer and less read (most of his books, in fact, are out of print) than he was a generation ago. His eclipsed reputation should not blind us to the freshness and pertinence of his religious vision. Silone was convinced that certain religious values have a perennial worth and a hidden life of their own. At times, these values are submerged by the predominant thought patterns of history, but they are recoverable in given circumstances. The circumstances may be very grave ones, but it takes only one person (or very few persons) to raise these values again for the larger populace. It may well be that the values (or the person who speaks them or lives them out) will appear strange or even repugnant to the populace at large. It is almost certain that they will be badly received by the powers of the world. There is religious precedent for this reaction. We have so canonized the Hebrew prophets, for example, that it is difficult for us to realize how badly people reacted to their message and their life. What Silone has argued, in the last analysis, is the persistence of the prophetic charism in the tradition of the saints. The saints, like the prophets of old, are people hard to identify and harder to identify with.

The struggle for such a sanctity is not only a struggle against the predominant forms of culture; it is also a struggle for the self, in the desire both to understand and to transcend that self. Faced with the enormity of total societies, whether they are explicitly dehumanizing or implicitly suffocating, there must be individuals who can overcome the limitations of self and situation. In a review of Graham Greene's recent novel *The Human Factor* (1978), Conor Cruse O'Brien made a telling point about the hero of the novel. Explicitly a nonbeliever, unable to affirm God, and unwilling to accept belief, Castle lived out a "hidden" Christian life in a darkly allusive way beyond his own powers of articulation. The hero, Castle, seems to have found his way to God through his maze of ambiguous, false, or silly messages, among these absurd, treacherous, or malevolent messengers. Is Castle finding his way to God, or is God finding his mysterious and darkly humorous way to Castle? Or is Castle perhaps in some sense already the residence of God, the Christ figure strangely moving among men? . . . There seems indeed to be a kind of inversion or diversion of Kafka, perhaps a Christianization: not just people in a quest of an inaccessible Castle, but the Castle itself engaged in a quest: man seeking Christ and Christ seeking men.[9]

The hero of *The Human Factor* is the most recent creation of Greene's entourage of souls who have attempted to make sense out of Christianity, which seems to be too demanding, too complex, and too rigid for simple humanity to live by. In this ongoing fictional meditation on faith in an age of God's eclipse (Greene, echoing Santayana, now describes himself as a "Catholic atheist"), there was one novel where Greene consciously tried to depict a new kind of saint: the unnamed priest in *The Power and the Glory* (1940). If Castle was a Christian *malgré lui*, the priest of *The Power and the Glory* was a saint who was canonized only by a simple coterie of faithful and the express desire of the novelist himself.

At first glance, it seems paradoxical, almost blasphemous, to think of Greene's priest as a saint. He was, after all, an alcoholic who had sired an illegitimate child. His life seems to be defined mostly by his lack of virtue; he was a self-professed coward and had a penchant for venality. Yet Greene makes it apparent that these moral blemishes do not begin to describe adequately the priest or the depths of his faith. By contrast, the novel's police lieutenant, who searches for the priest (the novel is set in the anticlerical period of pre–World War II Mexico), has all of the external characteristics of a genuine priest: He is staunchly celibate, totally controlled and dedicated to his work, living in monastic simplicity, and fiercely abstemious; and has an almost mystical sense of the world that is like the reverse of religious faith since he experienced "a complete certainty in the existence of a dying, cooling world, of human beings who had evolved from animals for no purpose at all."[10]

A few years before Graham Greene wrote *The Power and the*

Glory, he had visited Mexico and had published a travel book entitled *The Lawless Roads* (1939). In the 1950 edition of that book, Greene noted in the introduction that those interested could find the prototype of the whiskey priest of his novel in a conversation he records later in the book with an expatriate dentist, Roberto Fitzpatrick. Greene had asked the dentist (the prototype for Dr. Tench in the novel) about a priest who had been in the area hiding from the police." 'Oh,' " he said, " 'He was just what we call a whiskey priest.' " He had taken one of his sons to be baptized but the priest was drunk and insisted on naming him Birgitta. " 'He was little loss, poor man,' " the dentist continued, " 'but who can judge what terror and hardship and isolation may have excused him in the eyes of God.' "[11]

It was from the casual conversation that Greene found the germ for his novel. There is, however, another element in *The Lawless Roads* that most critics have overlooked. In that book, Greene describes an actual priest fugitive who died a martyr's death in Mexico some ten years before Greene wrote. Father Miguel Pro Juarez, S.J., was born in Concepcion del Oro in 1891. He entered the Jesuit order as a teenager but, due to the antireligious laws of Mexico, was sent by his superiors first to Spain and then to Belgium for his studies. After training in the social sciences, he was ordained and returned clandestinely to Mexico in 1926. Father Pro carried on a surreptitious ministry until 1927, when he was captured by the police. He was executed by a government firing squad on November 23, 1927.

With characteristic obtuseness, the police published a photograph of Padre Pro's execution in the newspaper and had it circulated on posters. The image of the handsome young priest, with arms outstretched before a bullet-pocked wall, became, as one might suspect, an instant holy card of a martyred saint. Greene reproduced the photo in *The Lawless Roads.* The photo was made illegal in Mexico, but the police had inadvertently canonized a saint by popular proclamation.

It is my contention that Padre Pro is the real antitype of the fictional whiskey priest in *The Power and the Glory;* but at the same time, both are saints in the novelist's estimation. The novel itself is

framed in the beginning and the end by a pious Mexican woman
reading to her children from a "holy book" about the exploits of a
Mexican priest martyr who had died during the persecution of the
Church. The recitation is filled with the pious moralisms standard in
hagiography: how he willingly left family, home, and country; his
rigorous mortifications; his prophetic interest in the Christian martyrs of old; and so on. The young boy who listens to these readings
at the beginning of the novel finds them silly and unconvincing; he
has a far greater interest in the exploits of Mexican patriots like
Pancho Villa, who evidence none of the simpering qualities of the
martyred priest. At the end of the novel, the mother is finishing her
reading about the martyr. The whiskey priest had just been executed
outside the village. The young boy begins to question his mother:

> "And that one," the boy said slowly, "The one they shot today. Was
> he a hero too?"
> "Yes"
> "He had a funny smell," one of the girls said.
> "You mustn't say that again," the mother said, "He may be one of
> the saints."
> "Shall we pray to him then?"
> The mother hesitated. "It would do harm. Of course, before we
> know he is a saint, there will have to be miracles. . . ."[12]

The great irony of the scene rests in the fact that the actual
priest's execution was nothing like those death scenes so common in
the hagiographical accounts. "Oh, no. Martyrs are not like me," said
the priest to his lieutenant captor, the night before the execution. "If
I had drunk more brandy I shouldn't be so afraid."[13] After the long
night of waiting for the coming dawn, the priest, bolstered somewhat
by a gift of brandy from the lieutenant, went unsteadily and fearfully
to his execution with an interior sense of abandonment, unrelieved
by any sense of consolation of faith or warmth of love:

> Tears poured down his face: he was not at the moment afraid of
> damnation—even the fear of pain was in the background. He felt only
> an immense disappointment because he had to go to God emptyhanded,
> with nothing done at all. It seemed to him at that moment that it would

have been quite easy to be a saint. It would have needed only a little
self-restraint and a little courage. He felt like someone who had missed
happiness by seconds at an appointed place. He knew now that at the
end there was only one thing that counted—to be a saint.[14]

It is obvious that in the mind of the author, this man is a saint.
In what did his sanctity consist? In the first place, whatever his
personal weaknesses might have been, he was a person of unshakable
supernatural faith. This deep faith was not something he willed; it
seized him and no matter how little he thought of himself, there was
always present this *prius* of belief. A child whom the priest meets,
after hearing him say that he could not renounce his faith since that
was beyond him, remarked that his faith must be like a birthmark—
it was just there and you had to get used to it.

This unworthy priest, marked by faith like a birthmark, was the
last priest left in his province. As he traveled, he sloughed off all of
the external appurtenances of his priesthood: The altar stone was too
cumbersome to carry; he lost his breviary; the chalice was gone; the
black suit was exchanged for the cast-off rags of a mestizo.[15] Beyond
that, he was conscious of his drinking, his illegitimate child, and the
ever present fear in the pit of his stomach. Despite these acts of
external loss, he never lost a sense of being a priest, even though it
was a sort of judgment on his own unworthiness: "After a time the
mystery became too great, a damned man putting God into the
mouths of men."[16]

This deep faith was ready to lead him to any sacrifice for the sake
of others. When he saw in his own little daughter that "the world
was in her heart like a small spot of decay on a piece of fruit," he
prayed, "Oh, God, give me any kind of death—without condition,
in a state of sin—only save this child."[17] The half-caste Judas who
would eventually be his betrayer kept the priest's confidence despite
his transparent treachery since, as the priest observed, "Christ died
for this man also."[18] As he looked at his betrayer, he "had given way
to despair—and out of that had emerged a human soul and love—
not the best love, but love all the same."[19] The priest's freedom was
ultimately lost because he went to give the Last Rites to an American

outlaw instead of fleeing the province as he had originally intended. After his death, the young boy who had dreamed of a revolutionary career after the pattern of Pancho Villa considered the priest a true hero and a saint. In a sense, the priest gave his life also for this young boy, since the last thing the boy does as the novel ends is to admit to the house a new priest who has just come to the area. The circle begins anew.

It was commonly charged a generation ago by some Catholic critics that Greene "sugarcoated" or "romanticized" sin. There was even some high-level criticism of him for his supposed "heterodox" views.[20] We need not rehearse these dreary charges or attempt to explain the general bewilderment that Catholics felt in the face of such works of fiction before the Council. What is evident, though, is that Greene was attempting to depict a saint in an entirely novel and radical way. Greene, an English convert well acquainted with the recusant priest martyrs of his own country, could well have employed a dashing hero after the manner of the Elizabethan martyrs of his own country. He had a precedent for such a person in the historical figure of Father Pro. What he did instead was to show a priest in all of his human loneliness and weakness with all of his disappointments and failures. Yet the reader reads the hero from the outside. Every time the priest voices his own sense of failure or unworthiness, the reader instinctively says "no" and affirms the contrary. The holiness of the priest wells up from a deep center of faith and engages everyone who meets him. In small gestures, he causes others to change. Even his persecutor is touched by contact with him. In that modest sense, his life was a paradigm and his death only furthered his influence.

Greene's most significant insight in this novel is that genuine saintliness comes when, in the midst of hostile and threatening cultural conditions, as every human instinct turns to self-interest and self-survival, a person can opt for transcendence and denial of self. It is interesting that in *The Power and the Glory,* every time the priest gets close to normal church conditions (with an appreciative village, for example), he becomes imperious and venal; in extremity (when he is in jail or on the run), he is stripped to the bare bones of faith and something in him responds to the clear impulse of God. Under normal circumstances, when a person shows his faith, forgives, or serves, he is pious or regular; when the same person acts in that fashion under strain and abnormal circumstances, the person comes close to sanctity. Castle, in Greene's *The Human Factor,* makes the point with precision: "There were priests I sometimes met in Africa who made me believe again—for a moment—over a drink. If all priests had been like they were and I had seen them often enough perhaps I would have swallowed the Resurrection, the Virgin Birth, Lazarus, the whole works."[21]

Both Silone and Greene have stripped Christianity (as a cultural system) down to its barest essentials in their novels. Silone has even removed the authentic sacramental character of his priest-hero. Greene's priest has that, but all of the moral and spiritual supports have been taken away. This nudity was obviously integral to the intentions of both novelists. The central religious problematic of both *Bread and Wine* and *The Power and the Glory* can be baldly stated: In what does heroic sanctity consist when it is left denuded of sympathetic support? The answer both authors have attempted to articulate is some sense of burning transcendence that sustains the hero and touches those few who come in contact with it.

Karl Rahner is famous for his prediction that in the future, Christianity will be in diaspora. His judgment about the future of Christianity may or may not be true, but it is quite clear that in certain places today it is already true and at certain moments in our recent historical past it has been an existent reality. Both Silone and Greene give us imaginative hints about what it would mean to be heroically Christian in a jail cell in present-day Paraguay or in the vast Gulags of the Soviet Union. The hidden saints who actually dwell there today only rarely get to speak to us about their actual condition; we have intimations of their life in a body of fiction that is now nearly forty years old. That fact alone keeps the Silones and the Greenes of our time from being dated.

Both Silone and Greene emphasize the pervasive inhumanity of repressive social structures as the background against which the spark of saintliness must be seen. These same social structures also reveal (indeed, they may derive from) what Martin Buber once called "the eclipse of God." The sense of God's loss and the nature of totalitarian structures are both vividly present in Albert Camus's novel, *The Plague* (1948). Most critics see the plague that spreads over the town of Oran in Algeria as a metaphorical description of Nazism's grip on wartime France. The hero of *The Plague*, Doctor Rieux, does not believe in God; but he struggles with all his might against the random violence of the plague that grips his city. In the course of the novel, Camus provides us with a profound meditation on living life with complete integrity but without any sense that life has any ultimate meaning. "Since the order of the world is shaped by death," said Doctor Rieux, "Mightn't it be better for God if we refuse to believe in Him and struggle with all our might against death, without raising our eyes towards the heaven where He sits in silence?"[22]

Unlike Rieux, his friend Tarrou cannot simply fight the plague with what Germaine Bree has called "the clear inner awareness of man's accidental and transitory presence on the earth."[23] That awareness causes metaphysical anguish; but Tarrou, more sensitive and less detached than Rieux, must combine awareness and sensitivity. Such a combination causes Tarrou to reach almost instinctively for the language of sanctity:

> "It comes to this," Tarrou said almost casually, What interests me is in learning how to become a saint."
> "But you don't believe in God?"
> "Exactly! Can one be a saint without God?—that's the problem, in fact, the only problem I'm up against today."
> . . . Tarrou said in a low voice that it was never over, and there would be more victims, because that was in the order of things.
> "Perhaps," the doctor answered. "But you know, I feel more fellowship with the defeated than with the saints. Heroism and sanctity don't really appeal to me, I imagine. What interests me is being a man."
> "Yes. We're both after the same thing, but I'm less ambitious."[24]

This thirst for sanctity, often articulated in modern culture, must not be dismissed as a literary conceit proffered by socially committed writers of a leftist tint. It would be unfair to say that what these

writers desire is a revolutionary figure motivated by some revolutionary passion analogous to religious sentiment. There is a whole literary
tradition, ranging from Dostoevsky and George Bernanos down to
contemporary writers like Walker Percy, who have written about the
place of the saint in modern culture. These novelists reflect the actual
situation of our times, which has produced, in the crucible of war,
violence, hostile regimes, and concentration camps, figures as luminous as Dietrich Bonhoeffer, Simone Weil, and Maximilian Kolbe.

The sanctity reflected in the novels I have discussed derives from
the fidelity of believers (or searchers) who pit their lives against an
openly hostile social environment. In all three novels, the pressures
against the life of grace are easy to identify and unashamedly implaca-
ble. The forthright militancy of antireligious governments is not the
only hostile environment for the emergence of heroic sanctity. It is
interesting to note that in the same period that Camus, Greene, and
Silone were writing their novels of antitotalitarianism, another novelist, George Bernanos, wrote a modern classic that looks at another
side of the modern problem of sanctity: *The Diary of a Country Priest*
(1936; later made into a splendid movie by Robert Bresson). The
hero of that novel, an unnamed country priest, is also clearly a saint.
He did not live either under the heel of Nazi Germany or in Fascist
Italy. His short adult life was passed in a rural village in prewar
France. His growth in sanctity did not derive from his struggles with
a militantly atheistic culture. His struggles were with the bourgeous
smugness and the peasant ignorance of his parishoners and his own
precarious health and recurring bouts of ennui and doubt. His whole
life is an endless cycle of daily tasks performed under the shadow of
the gnawing pain of an undiagnosed tumor. At his death, he is pitied
by cleric and laity alike as a well-meaning but ineffectual failure.
Through the whole fabric of the novel, however, we can trace the
faint transforming mark of his life as it touches the bitterness, cyni-
cism, and despair of others who come in contact with him.

The unnamed curé of George Bernanos represents the other side
of the hiddenness of the modern saint: heroic witness in the face of
indifference and despair. This kind of saint faces incomprehension
rather than hostility. His life is at odds with the prevailing temper

of the times. Contemporary novelists with religious preoccupations
—one thinks immediately of Flannery O'Connor and Walker Percy
—have been quite sensitive to the discrepancy between religious
witness and the prevailing culture. When once queried about the
startlingly bizarre religious characters that populate her fiction, Flannery O'Connor pungently observed that for the blind you write large
and for the deaf you shout.

What has been the fictive construction of the artist and the
existential reality of our many modern martyrs has also been the
subject of profound reflection on the part of our most capable
spiritual writers. It is germane to my thesis to recall that Thomas
Merton spent his mature years as a Trappist contemplative attempting to understand the search for holiness in light of our present
cultural situation. Merton was deeply sensitive to the secularizing
impulses in our world and the attendant horrors that are spawned
through those impulses. There is no doubt that anyone who thirsts
after a genuine contemplative life, even in the secure confines of
American culture, would have to pass through the modern experience
of living in this age. Our cultural suppositions and native attitudes
can no more be avoided than one can live and decide to suspend
breathing. The state of the "dark night of the soul"—the *noche
oscura* of John of the Cross—can now be understood in other, but
equally compelling, terms. Merton borrows from the existentialist
vocabulary when he sees the human condition today as circumscribed
by a sense of *dread:*

> Dread is an expression of our insecurity in this earthly life, a realiza-
> tion that we are never and can never be completely "sure" in the sense
> of possessing a definitive and existential spiritual status. . . . In other
> words we no longer rely on what we "have," what has been given by our
> past, what has been acquired. We are open to God and to his mercy in
> the inscrutable future and our trust is entirely in the emptiness where
> we will confront unforeseen decisions. Only when we have descended in
> dread to the center of our nothingness, by his grace and his guidance,
> can we be led by him, in his own time, to find him in losing ourselves.[25]

The dread of which Merton speaks should not be understood in only its most dramatic formulation. Many people do not experience the heavy sense of *Angst* so compellingly described by the existentialists. Nor are many persons in the comfortable world of the West put in the extreme social situations of the Gulag or the police detention center. Yet everyone is tested in those occasional microsituations that give quiet testimony to the omnipresence of personal dread. In fact, the dread of which Merton speaks in the quotation refers not only to the spiritual insecurities of the contemplative but to the normal anxieties of living a consciously reflective life. Walker Percy once caught it in a near perfect existentialist vignette: "A man comes home from work every day at five thirty to the exurbs of Montclair or Memphis and there is the grass growing and the little family looking not quite at him but just past the side of his head, and there's Cronkite on the tube and the smell of pot roast in the living room, and inside the house and outside in the pretty exurb has settled the noxious particles and the sadness of the old dying Western world, and him thinking: Jesus, is this it? Listening to Cronkite and the grass growing?"[26]

Merton's dread is, in the vocabulary of Walker Percy, "everydayness." In all of his major novels, Percy has hammered at the same basic theme: We are living in perilous times, made all the more perilous by the failure of scientific humanism and the blind complacencies of materialism. It is in that condition, personal and social, that the Christian message must be heard. Percy insists that the "Good News" in such a culture as ours may well up from hidden sources. Surveying not totalitarian society but the dying institutions of the West led Percy to depict the prophetic bearers of truth in startling but modest ways. In his futurist novel, *Love in the Ruins* (1971), one of the last of the old-fashioned priests (the one who reconciles the hero of the novel at the end of the book) is an "obscure curate, who remained faithful to Rome, who could not support himself and had to hire out as a fire watcher. It was his job to climb the firetower at night and watch for brush-fires below and for signs and portents in the skies."[27] That arresting description of the hidden prophet, the forgotten saint, the faithful watcher is seen by Percy as the one essential vocation for our time: "What with the present dislocation of man, it is probably an advantage to see man by his very nature an exile and a wanderer rather than as the behavourist sees him: as an organism in an environment. Despite Camus' explicit disavowal of Christianity, his Stranger has blood ties with the wayfarer of St. Thomas Aquinas and Gabriel Marcel. And if it is true that we are living in eschatological times, times of enormous danger and commensurate hope, of possible end and possible renewal, the prophetic-eschatological character of Christianity is peculiarly apposite."[28]

What Walker Percy has seen for Catholicism in general is not unlike what Merton has seen for the role of the monk in particular. One could say that Thomas Merton's lifelong reflection on the meaning of the monastic charism is a case study in *aggiornamento*. From 1941, when he entered the monastery, until 1968, when he died, Merton reflected on his monastic vocation. That vocation was tested, not only in the monastery itself but by the external pressures of a changing Church. In that twenty-seven-year period, Merton's understanding of what a monk is changed, but his conviction that he should be a monk never wavered. That was no mean accomplishment when one remembers the exodus from religious life in the 1960s because of the alleged "irrelevancy" or "unreality" of vowed communal existence. There is something profoundly ironic about Thomas Merton, a pacifist, civil rights advocate, antiwar activist, and social critic, making an energetic case for irrelevancy and marginality in the face of a near-unanimous 1960s cry for commitment, relevancy, and action.

Merton was a prolific writer; but when one looks at his writings, at least his major ones, one can see a definite evolution in his understanding of the monastic charism. His autobiography, *The Seven Storey Mountain* (1948), reflects a deep distaste for modern culture, a rigid view of the rightness of a "supernatural" vocation, a denigration of the world, and a harsh asceticism. In his later years, Merton was acutely conscous of how narrowly judgmental he had been in his earlier life. He himself parodied the early Merton as the "man who spurned New York, spat on Chicago, and tromped on Louisville, heading for the woods with Thoreau in one hand, John of the Cross in another, and holding the Bible open to the Apocalypse."[29]

Nor was Merton insensitive to the need for a deeper understanding of monastic life within the family of monasticism itself. His writings reflect—often obliquely—his unhappiness with the rigidity, conformity, and infantilism found in the monasteries. He himself— as we are now beginning to learn piecemeal—suffered a good deal at the hands of censors, superiors, and the system itself. There are open appeals in his last writings for change. He felt that resistance to change and reform was destroying vocations for younger monks and making life intolerable for the mature ones.

That combination of dissatisfaction with one's early religious convictions and frustration with actual ecclesiastical structures is a potent recipe for spiritual alienation. Yet Merton did not despair at the monastic life or fall into the comfortable dead end of fixing his attention exclusively on structural reform. He did, indeed, struggle for reform, but his best energies were kept for understanding anew what it meant to be a monk in a culture that had little patience for those who were not actively engaged in the world of action. For Merton, the task of being a monk in our age did not consist of doing this or that particular work. The monk was dedicated solely to being a man of God. He described the monk as "a marginal person who withdrew deliberately to the margin of society with a view of deepening fundamental human experience."[30] Merton, then, with a fine eye for irony, recognized that a monk in Kentucky, living a traditional life in a monastery, guided by an essentially traditional *ethos,* was not at the heart of action and was not meant to be. His task was to be faithful as a *monachus* (one alone), and in that simple fidelity, he would build up the church of Christ. In an extraordinary letter written to a Cistercian abbot in Italy in 1967, Merton summed up his understanding of the monastic life by addressing some words to a hypothetical "person in the world." It is a clear statement of what a monk is and how he might relate to the world:

> My flight from the world is not a reproach to you who remain in the world, and I have no right to repudiate the world in a purely negative fashion, because if I do that my flight will have taken me not to truth

and to God but to a private, though doubtless pious, illusion.

. . . My brother, perhaps in my solitude I have become as it were an explorer for you, a searcher in realms which you are not able to visit —except perhaps in the company of your psychiatrist. I have been summoned to explore a desert area of man's heart where explanations no longer suffice, and in which one learns that only experience counts. An arid, rocky, dark land of the soul, sometimes illumined by strange fires which men fear and peopled by spectres which men studiously avoid except in their nightmares. And in this area I have learned that one cannot truly know hope unless he has found out how like despair hope is.[31]

What Merton writes of the vocation of the monk is, *mutatis mutandis,* of application for a sanctity open to anyone in our time and in our culture. If the saint is one who sets forth for others a "new way of being Christian," it is likely that such an epiphany of being Christian is going to show up most clearly against a strongly contrasting background. Hence, a strong affirmation of the Incarnational values of Christ set against the dehumanization of the Gulag or a deep sense of wonder, freshness, and hope emanating from a smug culture of middle-class materialism is not only a judgment against the weakness of that culture but an arresting alternative to it. Almost by definition, this is going to be an individual effort against the majority consensus; it is its persistent quality of being imitable that makes it important. Not everyone is called to be a Trappist contemplative, but such a person living that life with utmost maturity and seriousness could, against a hostile larger background, illuminate the lives of others to seek out alternatives of life and spirituality. How are we to judge the impact of Merton's years of silence and prayer except in the light of the subsequent hope and encouragement the life he led gave to others? Who would have thought that the strange, intense, and hidden life of a Simone Weil, so apparently formless, chaotic, and unfinished, would touch generations after her obscure death in exile? How could the Soviet government have known that an obscure and obstinate political prisoner, hidden in the vast backwaters of the Gulag, would create a moral revolution in the area of political consciousness?

The persons surveyed in this chapter have been uniformly obscure. They range from the Silonian "solitary stranger" to the humble religious who inhabit the backwaters of Louisiana, Mexico, or rural France. They all share in that vast amorphous reality we call, with varying degrees of precision, modern society or mass culture or post-industrial civilization. They live out their lives in counterpoint to hostile or indifferent structures. We should not overdramatize this hiddenness; it can be as heroic as the resister's life in a totalitarian society or as banal as quotidian existence in the American exurbs described by Walker Percy. Modern sanctity reveals itself almost as a surprise, a surprise either at the kind of person who shows us the saintly life or surprise at where that person comes from: A secretary general of the United Nations a mystic? An alcoholic priest in the dusty provinces of Mexico a saint? A poor wretch in the next cell a friend of God? The family in the adjacent suburban tract house true servants of God? That may well be the character of modern sanctity. The late theologian and spiritual writer, Romano Guardini, has attempted a delineation of this kind of sanctity. His description is right in line with what I have tried to articulate in this chapter:

> Their surroundings are standardized: they live in laboratories, in factories, in administrative agencies . . . live in homes which are often the same in the smallest detail . . . dress the same . . . are subject to uniform "packages" of education, entertainment, legislation. In such an environment, how could they lead a Christian way of life which had to express itself in extraordinary religious practices and experiences? They would have to become strangers to their own way of existence. They themselves would have to recognize their lives as absurdities.[32]

Traditional Christian hagiography has often pointed with pride to the witness of the humble lay brother, the simple extern sister, the obscure hermit, or the pious gatekeeper whose fidelity and asceticism has had far-reaching influence on the Christian life of the larger world. The "little way" of Saint Thérèse of Lisieux had a powerful impact on the spirituality of the Catholic Church. That Thérèse was the patroness of world missions, though she herself lived out her life in a French Carmel in the last century, is witness to the power of the hidden life as an energizer of spiritual power. The unnamed wanderer of the nineteenth-century Russian spiritual classic *The Way of the Pilgrim* presents a similar case.

Such examples could be multiplied. The "hiddenness" of sanctity is a persistent theme in the history of spirituality. What seems to be different today is that those who have spoken most compellingly of that theme have found their place of speaking not in the familiar cultural oases of a monastery or the other locations of Christian culture but in prisons, camps, deserts, or even in the brittle sterility of middle-class neighborhoods. What is even more striking is that some who do not pledge any formal allegiance to the institutional Church—Greene, Silone, and Camus have been my examples—witness to the need for such hidden sanctity in the face of a hostile culture. These hidden saints, real and imagined (hagiography is full of real and imagined saints) pronounce judgments on our era and call for a new announcement of the Good News. They carry in their lives the mustard seed, the pinch of leaven, the small coin; and in their lonely pilgrimage, they scatter them on the surface of our dead winter world.

NOTES

1. Dag Hammarskjöld, *Markings* (New York: Knopf, 1964), p. 122.
2. Richard L. Rubenstein, *The Cunning of History* (New York: Harper and Row, 1975).
3. Pierre Hassner, "Western European Perceptions of the USSR," *Daedalus* (Winter 1979), pp. 113–150.
4. Theodore Ziolkowski, *Fictional Transfigurations of Jesus* (Princeton: Princeton University Press, 1972), pp. 55–97. Ziolkowski's study builds on earlier works: R. W. B Lewis, *The Picaresque Saint* (Philadelphia: Lippincott, 1959); Cleanth Brooks, *The Hidden God* (New Haven: Yale University Press, 1963); R. M. Frye, *Perspective on Man* (Philadelphia: Westminster, 1961). At about the same time these scholarly discussions were going on, the novelist J. D. Salinger was exploring the notion of sainthood in American culture in *Franny and Zooey* (Boston: Little, Brown, 1962) and *Raise High the Roof Beam, Carpenters* and *Seymour, An Introduction* (Boston: Little, Brown, 1963).
5. Ignazio Silone, *Bread and Wine* (New York: Signet Classic, 1962), p. 30.
6. Ibid., p. 270.
7. From the introduction to Silone's play, *And He Hid Himself* (New York:

Harper and Row, 1945). For a study of this theme, see Robert McAfee Brown, "Ignazio Silone and the Pseudonyms of God." In Harry Mooney and Thomas Staley, eds., *The Shapeless God: Essays on Modern Fiction* (Pittsburgh: University of Pittsburgh Press, 1968), pp. 19–40.

8. Silone, *And He Hid*, pp. 62–63.

9. Conor Cruse O'Brien, "Greene's Castle," *The New York Review of Books* (June 1, 1978), p. 4.

10. Graham Greene, *The Power and the Glory* (New York: Viking, 1940), p. 20.

11. I have studied this issue in greater depth in Lawrence S. Cunningham, "The Alter Ego of Greene's Whiskey Priest," *English Language Notes* (September 1970), pp. 50–52.

12. Greene, *The Power*, p. 211.

13. Ibid., p. 186.

14. Ibid., pp. 199–200.

15. This theme is remarkably like that of the priest in Luis Buñuel's powerful film *Nazarin* (1951); both works are set in Mexico.

16. Greene, *The Power*, p. 56.

17. Ibid., p. 76.

18. Ibid., p. 92.

19. Ibid., p. 94.

20. Compare Francis Kunkel, *The Labyrinthine Ways of Graham Greene* (New York: Sheed and Ward, 1959) for an earlier Catholic account of these discussions.

21. Cited in O'Brien, "Greene's Castle." Greene's *The Human Factor* was published in 1978 (New York: Simon and Schuster).

22. Albert Camus, *The Plague* (New York: Vintage Paperback, 1963), p. 121.

23. Germaine Bree, *Albert Camus* (New York: Harcourt Brace Jovanovich, 1961), p. 122.

24. Camus, *The Plague*, pp. 237–238.

25. Thomas Merton, *Contemplative Prayer* (Garden City: Doubleday Image, 1971), p. 101.

26. Walker Percy, "Bourbon," *Esquire* (December 1975), p. 148.

27. Walker Percy, *Love in the Ruins* (New York: Dell Paperback, 1972), p. 6.

28. Walker Percy, "Notes for a Novel About the End of the World." In *The Message in the Bottle* (New York: Farrar, Strauss, and Giroux, 1975), p. 111.

29. Thomas Merton, *Contemplation in a World of Action* (Garden City: Doubleday Image, 1973), p. 159.

30. Thomas Merton, *Asian Journal* (New York: New Directions, 1973), p. 305.

31. Thomas Merton, "A Letter on the Contemplative Life." In Patrick Hart, ed., *The Monastic Journey* (Garden City: Doubleday Image, 1978), pp. 220–221.

32. Romano Guardini, *The Saints in Ordinary Christian Life* (Philadelphia: Chilton, 1966), p. 77–78.

CHAPTER 5

Saintliness and the Desert

IN THE previous chapters, I have argued that our times demand, and have produced, a new sanctity—one that is characterized by its hiddenness. This hidden sanctity reveals itself against the background of hostile or indifferent environments. To argue that our age demands a new sanctity is not to say that it is a sanctity discontinuous with the past. In fact, I have made a quite different argument: The saint manifests both the perennial value of the Gospel and a new and enduring way of fleshing out that vision in life.

There is nothing contradictory or even paradoxical about linking innovation and tradition. Christianity is, after all, a tradition that lives itself out in the unfolding of history. Christianity takes its stand on the historical revelation of a Person at a particular moment in history; it lives itself out as the unfolding of the meaning of that personal revelation. For that reason, every attempt at Church reform or religious renewal is, in the first place, a renewed scrutiny of the wellsprings of Christianity itself. There is a continuous thread of images and symbols that runs from the first proclamation of the Gospel right down to the present day. The manner in which those images and symbols are grasped depends on cultural conditions and historical sentiments. The Orphic Christ of the early Christian sarcophagi, the Byzantine mosaics of the *Pantocrator*, and the touching babies of Botticelli or Raphael are all partial attempts to articulate the "Word made Flesh."

Consider the following texts on religious poverty:

> Take
> no gold
> nor silver,
> nor copper in your belts,
> no bag for your journey,
> nor two tunics,
> nor sandals,
> nor a staff
>
> (MATT. 10:9–10)

One of the monks, called Serapion, sold his book of the Gospels and gave the money to those who were hungry, saying: I have sold the book which told me to sell all that I had and give it to the poor.[1]

(Sayings from the Desert Fathers)

No brother is to accept or solicit money. A brother should never even accompany those who beg for money. He can take any other form of recompense except that one. When there is an urgent necessity a brother can get money for someone needy like a leper but he should handle money even then with reluctance.

(ST. FRANCIS OF ASSISI, *The Rule of 1221*)

If you desire to be perfect, sell your will, give it to the poor in spirit, come to Christ in meekness and humility, and follow Him to Calvary and the sepulcher.

(ST. JOHN OF THE CROSS, *Spiritual Maxim*)

> You want to be,
> excuse me,
> First get free
> of that excess
> of goods
> which cram
> your whole body
> leaving no room
> for you and even less
> for God.
>
> (DOM HELDER CAMARA,
> *The Desert Is Fertile*)

Each of these texts speaks of evangelical poverty. They all reflect, in one way or another, the Gospel command "to travel light," that is, to be detached from the things of this world in order to ensure the freedom of the Gospel. Yet each of those texts, seen in its specific context, speaks to a peculiar historical moment in the life of the Church.

We have such easy access to the printed word that it is only in historical context that we understand how heroic a gesture it was for Abbot Serapion to sell his Gospel codex. Both Saint Francis of Assisi in the thirteenth century and Bishop Helder Camara in the twentieth show a passionate concern for poverty. Saint Francis wanted a money-free style of life for his brothers and legislated rather minutely how money was to be avoided. Bishop Camara, by contrast, lives today in northern Brazil and his concern is the vast disparity between the rich and the poor in our contemporary world. His slant on poverty is that of a Third World person who thinks that the gross materialism of Western culture strangles the spirituality necessary to bring about a just social order. His message is as old as the prophets and the Gospels and as contemporary as the headlines of today's newspaper. Saint John of the Cross, by contrast, has interiorized the concept of poverty in order to pursue his vocation as a mystic and contemplative.[1]

The entire history of Christian spirituality can be seen as the story of discerning how to live out the perennial message of the Gospel in the here and now. Are there themes peculiar to a certain age? One could probably make such a case, but only at the risk of indulging in those vast generalizations to which historians are somewhat prone. We speak rather sweepingly of the "Age of Faith" or the "Age of Evangelization." When we look more closely at the tradition of the saints, we see less a class of persons who exemplify this or that virtue in a given age and more individuals who give new meaning to a particular aspect of the Gospel message. In his study of biography and theology, James William McClendon has argued—to cite just a few instances—that the late Martin Luther King, Jr., gave new meaning to the Exodus motif of the Bible and Dag Hammarskjöld personified the "servant" ideal of the Gospel.[2]

One theme that has had a continuing presence in the entire

tradition of Christian spirituality is the spiritual significance of the desert. Precisely because the desert conjures up first impressions so apparently alien to the concerns of life in the largely urban culture of the West, I propose to trace that theme down to our present age in order to show that the perennial value of the desert tradition has persisted to our present day in forms that are both traditional and new.

Deserts are mentioned about three hundred times in the Bible. The Hebrew word for desert *(midbār)* comes from a semitic root that means "to drive animals to pasture." In the original sense of the term, then, the desert was any desolate area that provided grass for pasturage during a brief rainy period but could not sustain cultivation or tillage on a regular or annual basis. Deserts are characteristic of the land found to the east and south of Jerusalem; it is a land, in the words of Jeremiah, "which is not sown" (Jer. 2:2).

More specifically, in the Bible, the desert consists of those barren wastes (the Negev comes immediately to mind) where there is little indication of vegetation. It is an area "unhabited and impassable, a land of drought, and the image of death . . . a land where no man walked and no man dwells" (Jer. 2:6). Various descriptions in the Bible paint an unflattering picture of this no-man's land (Job 38:26), where venemous serpents dwell (Isa. 30:6) and thorns and briars thrive (Judg. 8:7).

As is true in many cultures, these desert wastelands were seen by the ancients as the dwelling place of evil and malignant spiritual forces. Jesus himself expressed this common attitude toward the desert wastelands when he noted that "when an unclean spirit has gone out of a man, he roams through dry places in search of rest and finds none" (Matt. 12:43).

It is in the stark harshness of the Sinai Desert that the People of Israel were tested and purified by God after they had been called out of Egypt. Indeed, much of the Exodus sojourn in the Wilderness is conceived as a series of contrasts between the remembered "flesh-pots" of Egypt and the unforgivingly harsh life of the desert. In the later history of Israel, the desert experience was seen as decisive in the formation of the People of God. The prophet Hosea depicted the desert sojourn as a rite of passage—a revelatory purification—that gave God the chance to speak to the hearts of His children in silence before returning them to the areas where there were the fertile lands of the vineyards and the orchards (Hos. 2:17). Both the Psalmist and the prophets stressed the absolute dependence of the flock of Israel in the desert on the guiding wisdom of their Shepherd who was God. For Deutero-Isaiah, the desert journey of the Exodus was an absolute sign of liberation. Yahweh himself constructed the road through the desert for His people (Isa. 43:19) and caused water to spring from barren rocks for their sustenance (Isa. 43:20).

There is, then, beneath the biblical idea of the desert, a dialectical understanding of the significance of the desert: It is a place without God (indeed, it is a place of malignant forces), but God leads people to it and helps them sustain themselves in that environment and strengthens them against the malignant forces of the desert. It is in that dialectical relationship between God and non-God that the story of the temptation of Jesus in the desert must be understood. Jesus was "driven by the Spirit (Mark 1:12) into the desert, where he fasted and prayed for forty days while "tempted by Satan and living amidst wild beasts" though "angels ministered to Him" (Mark 1:13). This story, elaborated both by Matthew (4:1–11) and Luke (4:1–13), is set at the beginning of the ministry of Christ. Like the Children of Israel, Jesus combats the demonic harshness of the desert as a prelude to going out from the desert with a mind set fully on his preaching.

The temptation of Christ in the desert traditionally has been linked to the subsequent development of Christian spirituality. The desert experience of the average Christian in the *imitatio Christi* is the observance of Lent, with its emphasis on fasting, self-abnegation, and silence. Jesus, we are reminded, was tempted and overcame temptation. The desert, then, if one wishes to use a spiritual short-hand, is the meeting of God in solitude through the experience of the harshness involved in the subjection of the self. It is not mere rhetoric that John the Baptist, the "greatest of men born of woman," as Jesus described him, should describe himself as the "voice of one crying out in the wilderness" (Matt. 3:3). John, as it were, came forth from the desert having encountered God and His message there.

The desert metaphor in the Bible goes even deeper than its use in verbal expressions. In a recent study, Herbert Schneidau has pointed out that the desert in the Near East "plays a part in the history of the Near East that uncannily sets the role of great opposites, enhancing and threatening man's life at the same time."[3] This fact is true not only at the level of political stability (deserts provide barriers for keeping other people at a distance), social style (one finds more nomads than tillers in desert regions), or alimentary habits, but also in the realm of the mythic and the religious. Some scholars argue, for example, that it was the shaping force of the desert landscape that contributed decisively to the development of the radical monotheism of Israel:

> In fact, he [the desert dweller] gains his freedom at the cost of significant form. For, wherever we find reverence for the phenomenon of life and growth, we find preoccupation with the immanence of the divine and with the form of its manifestation. But in the stark solitude of the desert, where nothing changes, nothing moves (except man at his own free will), where features in the landscape are only pointers, landmarks, without significance in themselves—there we might expect the image of God to transcend concrete phenomena altogether.[4]

Commenting on this observation, Herbert Schneidau pointed out that for those who lived by such a desert (whether in the Near East or in Don Juan's Mexico), it is not a question of living next to lifelessness or dead landscapes; it is, rather, life in an environment "charged" with sources of power; with the possibility of hierophany and kratophany—the emergence of both the sacred and evil. There is a tension in the desert experience; it is an experience of silence, solitude, and of monochrome (or polychrome) formlessness with sudden eruption of inexplicable power.[5]

It is against the background of this understanding of the desert that we must view the lives of the early Christian solitaries in Palestine and Egyptian Thebiad. They form a sort of spiritual kindship with the Essenian desert dwellers, who lived out their lives in conscious imitation of the Children of Israel who had gone out into the desert in obedience to the promises of God. The *homines spirituales* who fled the provincial cities of the Roman Empire in the fourth century to seek God in the desert are the forerunners of the entire monastic tradition of Christianity. The most famous memoir of this period, *The Life of Saint Anthony* by Saint Athansius, is filled with descriptions of Saint Anthony's search for God and his temptations with the demonic powers of the desert. These evil forces not only come in the form of seductive phantasms (beautiful women who attempt to seduce him or equally sensual images of food, drink, warmth, and such), but also in terms of the malign elements of the desert itself: "It was indeed remarkable that, though alone in such a wilderness, he was not frightened away by the demons that attacked him, nor alarmed at the wildness of the four footed beasts and creeping things, although, they were numerous, but he truly trusted the Lord like Mount Sion, as the Scripture says, with a serene and tranquil mind, so that the demons fled instead, and the wild beasts kept peace with him, as it is written."[6] Anthony, in response to those temptations, sought greater solitude and more austerity together with less reliance on material encumbrances—all characteristics of the "desert personality." Saint Athanasius depicted Anthony as finally emerging from his experience as a victor over temptation, the desert, and the self; as such, he became a paradigm for other ascetics. Athansius then goes on to describe the effect of this life as a blooming of the desert with urban evils vanquished. The desert becomes a peaceful kingdom and an anticipation of the concord of heaven:

> And truly one could see a land set apart, as it were—a land of piety and justice. For neither wrongdoer or wronged was there, nor complaint of the tax collector, but of a great number of ascetics, all of one mind towards virtue. As one looked again on the cells and on the regularity of the monks, one cried aloud saying: How beautiful are thy tabernacles, O Jacob, thy tents, O Israel! As wooded valleys, as watered gardens near the rivers: as tabernacles which the Lord has pitched: as cedars by the waterside (Num. 24:5–6).[7]

This struggle of the holy individual (whether alone or in community) in the desert has persisted as a style of life from Anthony's day down to the present. Besides the historical continuity of an orthodox

monastery like Saint Catherine's in the Sinai, there has been any
number of experiments based on the desert ideal. As many scholars
have pointed out, when it was no longer possible to go out into the
desert in some physical way, the concept of the desert was internal-
ized either by the creation of an artificial desert or by conceptualizing
an interior desert of the heart. Medieval monastic orders like the
Carthusians and the Camaldolese attempted to construct a desert in
their monasteries. The Carmelite Friars of the Middle Ages started
as an eremetical group after Saint Simon Stock (died 1265) visited
and lived with some Christian solitaries who had lived on Mount
Carmel in the Holy Land. The first Carmelite foundation in Europe
(Aylesford in Kentish England) was based on the solitary desert ideal;
and even after a shift to the mendicant style of wandering and
begging, the Carmelites still stressed the desert ideal. Contemporary
Carmelites still maintain "deserts" for retirement into a life of prayer,
solitude, and meditation. Even Saint Francis of Assisi (died 1224),
the most peripathetic of medieval saints, retired to desert places (for
example, the Carceri above Assisi and Mount Alverno, where he
received the stigmata) for periods of solitude and prayer. Saint Bona-
venture wrote his famous *Mind's Journey to God* at Mount Alverno
some years later and subtitled that work "The Meditation of a Poor
Man in the Desert." This inclination for the eremetical life remained
a constant in Franciscanism; indeed, among the Spiritual Franciscans, it became a priority as one way of protesting the intellectual
urbanity of the Conventionals, who had gone to the towns and to
university lectureships. The fourteenth-century Franciscans of the
Italian Marches were largely eremetical; their life is somewhat reflected in the *Fioretti*, a work heavily influenced by the ideas of the
more rigorous of the Franciscans.

The history of monasticism in the West derives from the tradition of the Desert Fathers. Within that tradition, the solitary ideal,
seen either as the physical living out of the eremetical ideal or the
psychological state of spiritual solitude, was maintained and promul-
gated. When one looks closely at the spiritual tradition of the West,
it is easy to see that some of its most innovative and powerful spiritual
masters—its saints—were deeply touched by the desert call. I have

already noted that Saint Francis of Assisi felt the need for solitary retirement as an intrinsic part of his spiritual program. It is easy to forget that this tug of the desert is behind even the most activist of Christian movements. Saint Ignatius Loyola (1491–1556), the founder of the Jesuits, spent a year in solitude in the caves of Manresa shortly after his religious conversion and just before he began his active life of pilgrimage and study. It was in the silences of Manresa in the mountains near the abbey of Monserrat that he wrote the first draft of the guide that was to shape the character of the most imginative religious movement of the post-Reformation Church: *The Spiritual Exercises.*

In the Eastern Orthodox Church, always sympathetic to the eremetical ideal, the idea of the person who retires from active life for the solitary ideal is best represented by the Orthodox notion of the Elder (in Greek, *geron*, in Russian, *staretz*). These religious are those spiritual masters of Orthodoxy who after a "long and vigorous preparation in solitude, having gained the gifts of discernment which are required of an elder, can open the door of their cell and admit the world from which they formerly fled."[8] The most famous of these holy men is the fictional *staretz,* Father Zosima in Dostoevsky's *The Brothers Karamazov.* Patterned after an actual *staretz* who lived at Optina monastery in the last century, Father Zosima is a spokesman for Dostoevsky's view that only a passionate faith in Christ would save Russia from the disasters that threatened it and, by extension, the world.

At the heart of the desert experience is solitude. This solitude expresses itself and is experienced in many ways and is reflected in quite diverse personal life stories in the story of Christian spirituality. The present-day hermits of Mount Athos look back to the prophet Elijah as a prototype just as the modern-day retreatant holds the image of Christ in the desert before his or her imaginative eye. The pursuit of solitude is, in the last analysis, an attempt to have some small experience of the absolute transcendence of God. The absolute symbol of that religious solitude is the desert. In solitude, saints both modern and ancient testify; people come closest to the immensity of God. Perhaps that is why the desert has been such a crucial element in the development of Christian spirituality. No single figure has ever expressed the paradoxical character of emptiness and fulness better than the great Spanish mystic, Saint John of the Cross. Every saint who has experienced the desert has testified to the rightness of his language, albeit in less poetic and paradoxical language:

> In this nakedness the soul finds
> its quietude and rest.
> For in desiring nothing,
> nothing raises it up
> and nothing weighs it down,
> because it is in the center of its humility.
> When it covets something
> In that very desire it is wearied.
>   (*The Ascent of Mt. Carmel,* I, 13)

This desire for solitude—the life of the desert—has been a persistent theme of Christian spirituality well beyond the Middle Ages. One can legitimately inquire if such a style of life is possible—or, better—desirable in our contemporary period. The late Thomas Merton, one of the more articulate defenders of the eremetical ideal, put the problem succinctly:

> In recent years some curious theories have been proposed which, in order to emphasize the importance of an active turning to the world and a "secular Christianity" have felt it necessary at the same time to discredit monastic solitude. The "contemplative life" of the monk is then discovered to be "Greek rather than Christian." The struggle with temptation in the wilderness is seen as a curious relic of gnosticism or some other heresy. Solitude is declared essentially alien to the Christian message and life which are communal. In a word, the whole monastic idea becomes theologically suspect.[9]

Whatever the validity of these *caveats,* it does seem clear that when one looks at twentieth-century Christian culture, there has been a persistence (indeed, a renewed interest) in keeping the desert ideal alive in the various monastic families of our times. Both Catholic Monasticism and that of Orthodoxy have maintained the eremetical idea. But beyond the traditional monastic usage, the desert ideal has been the source and inspiration of some truly innovative experiments in religious living as well as the source of some daring and creative theologizing. Charles de Foucauld (1858–1916), deeply touched by desert experiences both before and after his conversion, created the only truly innovative religious order of modern Catholicism as a result of his lived experience in the deserts of North Africa. Pierre Teilhard de Chardin (1891–1955), never a monk (he was a Jesuit priest) and only *per accidens* a desert solitary (he spent much time in the desert because of his scientific work), made the most audacious attempt at a new and total vision of Christianity, which was cosmic in its range. That vision was, as we shall see, developed from his own sense of the vastness and mystery of the world as he experienced it during his long periods of solitude in the Gobi Desert.

Charles de Foucauld was born in France to wealth and title.[10] Raised by an indulgent grandfather after the death of his parents when he was six, Charles led one of those lives that are of the stuff of nineteenth-century novels: an abortive military education at the academy of Saint Cyr; a generous inheritance, which he squandered as a cavalry lieutenant; departure for Algeria (in the company of his mistress) for some military action to shake off his sense of boredom; and abandonment of his *bon vivant* style of life after his profound encounter with Islamic culture while in North Africa. In 1882, he resigned from the army after having already made an intensive study of Islamic culture and the Arabic language. In 1883, Charles de Foucauld made an extensive exploration of the yet unexplored interior of Morocco. He crossed the desert stretches with caravans while disguised as a Jewish merchant, since westerners were suspect and forbidden in the area. His explorations won him the gold medal of the French Geographical Society in 1885, and his published report of his journey (*Reconnaissance au Maroc*—1888) was a recognized scientific classic of the time.

In the period between his Morocco exploration and the publication of the *Reconnaissance,* Charles de Foucauld went through an intense religious crisis. This crisis seems to have been precipitated by a combination of factors: the extremely devout example of his cousin, Madame Marie de Bondy; his own memories of the austerely devout religion of the Moslems that he had known in North Africa; and the fine spiritual advice he received from the Abbé Huvelin, a priest in Paris who numbered among his spiritual clients the composer Gounod, the scientist Pasteur, and the famous student of mysticism Baron Von Hügel. The resolution of this intense period of spiritual searching came when de Foucauld was received back into the Catholic Church (this was in 1888) after many years of religious indifference and spiritual estrangement. It was not surprising, given his rather passionate temperament, that Charles de Foucauld capped his return to the faith by entering the Trappist monastery of Notre Dame des Neiges the following year and then transferring to the order's daughter foundation at Cheikhle in Syria.[11]

From 1889 to 1897, Brother Marie Alberic (his name in religion) lived as a Trappist; his life was punctuated by a period of study in Rome and a constant struggle with his sense of vocation. He was sure there was a way to live a life of greater austerity and hiddenness than what could be provided within the confines of the Trappists, even though he had originally chosen the monastery of Notre Dame des Neiges because of its reputation for poverty and the austerity of its observance. De Foucauld left the Trappists in 1897 to take up residence as a gardener and handyman for some Poor Clare nuns at their enclosed convent in Nazareth. This experience, given over as it was to a life of humble work, prayer, and solitude, gave him a deep desire for what he called the "hidden life of Nazareth," that is, he wanted to be as hidden as the Christ before his public manifestation that initiated the public ministry.

It was also during this time that Charles de Foucauld began to dream of a new kind of religious order. Events began to move quickly and in a way that gave him the chance to test out these ideas. He returned to France, prepared for the priesthood, and was finally ordained in 1901. Soon after his ordination, Charles left for Algeria and set up a hermitage at Beni Abbes at the edge of the Sahara. He hoped, by the simplicity of his life, to be a witness for Christ who would be a sign both for the native Moslem population and the French *colons* who then ruled Algeria. He remained at Beni Abbes until 1905, when he decided to move farther into the desert. He traveled into the interior of the country to the area mainly inhabited by the fierce nomadic people, the Tuaregs. He built his hermitage at the oasis of Tamanrasset and remained there, with the exception of those times he journeyed to France, for the rest of his life. He never did gain any companions to live the religious life with him, and he had few apostolic successes as a missionary of witness. In 1916, during a rebellion of native tribesmen, a group of rebels came to his hermitage. The natives ordered him out of his hermitage, and a fifteen-year-old boy who was guarding him shot and killed him outside his home. De Foucauld died without having made a convert or attracting a single novice to his desert outpost.

In 1909, on a visit to France, Charles de Foucauld had a rule of life for his proposed religious society (The "Union of Brothers and Sisters of the Sacred Heart") approved by local religious authorities. At his death, no brother had come to join him and no sister had indicated a willingness to take up his way of life. In 1916, the year of his death in the remote backcountry of North Africa, the proposed order seemed to be stillborn. In 1933, however, Father Rene Voillaume, a Marseilles priest, started a religious order founded on the ideals of Charles de Foucauld in the Sahara. This order has had a steady growth over the years and an influence in the Church far in excess of its numbers. The famous philosopher, Jacques Maritain, was long associated with it and actually ended his days as a member of its fraternity. In 1968, the Little Brothers and Sisters of Jesus was large enough to be placed under the Vatican as a religious order of papal jurisdiction. They are not just one more religious order; they have taken the ancient ideal of the desert and reapplied it to the peculiar needs of our age.

Instead of building monasteries or convents, the Little Brothers and Sisters live in the midst of the world to experience poverty, not as something willed and acted out, but as something shared and part of the environment. Hence, a fraternity of brothers might live in an industrial slum, with a caravan of gypsies, or in a poor village. The brothers work for a living, not by pottering about in a monastery garden, but in petrochemical factories or as farm laborers. They balance the life of work with the life of prayer in the fraternity. In other words, they seek to fulfill the old Benedictine dictum of "work and pray" in the heart of the world. They deliberately choose those places in our culture that are the poorest or the most alienated in order to make the presence of God felt where His existence seems most problematical or senseless. They are not aggressive missionaries or proselytizers; they are contemplatives who seek to create a climate of spiritual presence and prayer.

The most important insight the Little Brothers and Sisters have given us is a new understanding of the notion of the desert in Christian spirituality. The United States today is dotted with retreat houses, houses of prayer, and places of solitude that attempt to recreate a "desert" environment for fostering the life of prayer and contemplation. Often as not, such establishments are reconverted dude ranches or the like situated in the picturesque canyons of the Southwest, where retreatants can recover a sense of silence and solitude. What the Little Brothers and Sisters have shown is that the deserts of our time are not natural environments but products of industrial culture. What, to cite an obvious example, manifests the greater sense of desolation, the Sangre de Cristo Mountains of New Mexico or the South Bronx? What is the difference between the lifelessness of the Sonora Desert and the daily life of the sweatshop? In a recent television series on the religions of the world (the PBS production, "The Long Search"), the segment on Roman Catholicism showed the Little Brothers who live in a working-class housing project in Leeds, England, while supporting themselves by working in a petrochemical plant in the area. That was the other side of their life; their novitiate included retreats in a natural desert area. The implication of the film was clear enough: The deserts are not made only by nature.

This "rereading" of the idea of the desert is an attempt to take an old ascetic ideal and see it in terms of the present historical situation. The spirituality of Charles de Foucauld was, in many ways, quite traditional; it was centered on the adoration of the Eucharistic Christ in silence and a keenly felt devotion to the Sacred Heart of Jesus. His metaphorical language is filled with imaginative meditations on the hidden life of Nazareth. But what is more important is that out of those traditional roots came a way to interpret old ideas into new ways of being. His spirituality was seen as a point of departure for new ways of being Christian.

However traditional the language and religious imagery of de Foucauld's spirituality may appear to us today, it is clear that one of his biographer's judgments is not far off the mark: "His vocation was entirely individual, absolutely new in the church, almost, as it were, conceived especially for him."[12] The witness of that unique life provided the inspiration for truly innovative ways of living out the religious life. A generation ago the Little Brothers outflanked the objections of the Vatican to the worker-priest experiments in France by their combination of humble labor and deeply centered contemplative activity. Likewise, the Little Sisters, in the very hiddenness of their lives, demonstrated a creative understanding of the traditional counsels of religious life. Their very humble and hidden style of life has had its own prophetic edge. Some years ago a group of the sisters in this country found employment among a much neglected group of workers: the charwomen who cleaned the offices and classrooms of a prominent Catholic college in the Northeast. Today small groups of these same religious live and work among people as disparate (and despised) as the gypsies of Europe or the slum dwellers of Latin America. A recent group of sisters has even begun living, for extended periods of time, with female prisoners.

Given their orientation and their understanding of the "new deserts" of the world, it is inevitable that the spiritual heirs of Charles de Foucauld would find a natural sympathy for the Third and Fourth World. Less political and activist than some of their Christian confreres, they are, nonetheless, providing an important spiritual dimension to the debates over liberation theology. Some of these contemporary brothers have gained a measure of popularity as spiritual writers. Carlo Carretto, who lives as a Little Brother in the Sahara, has published a series of studies on the desert experience as it relates both to the Christian social conscience and religious transcendence.[13] His confrere, Arturo Paoli, lives in Argentina; his recent published works have combined a deep contemplative spirit with a programmatic outline of social and religious reform.[14]

Pierre Teilhard de Chardin (1881–1955), Jesuit priest, renowned paleontologist, scientist, and spiritual writer, is one of the most attractive and controversial personalities of modern Catholicism. Later I shall speak about the originality of his spiritual vision; here I must mention his desert experiences. Like de Foucauld, Teilhard de Chardin went to the desert willingly; but unlike de Foucauld, his purpose in doing so was not primarily ascetic. In 1923, a year after his appointment as professor of geology at the *Institut Catholique* in Paris, he went to China as a member of a scientific expedition. From that base in China, he made a number of scientific trips to Mongolia and spent time in the vast reaches of the Gobi Desert; it was an expedition that would last until the end of 1924. The published letters of that period speak of his scientific work, his observations on the physical and cultural characteristics of the regions he visited, and the work he was doing. More significantly for our purposes, he saw all of these things in the light of his own deepening mystical vision of the world: "The more I look into myself," he wrote to his friend and professional colleague, Abbé Breuil, "the more I find myself possessed by the conviction that it is only the science of Christ running through all things, that is to say the mystical science, that really matters."[15]

It was out of this rather dialectical cauldron of empirical scientific research and his own mystical sense that Teilhard composed his contemplative meditation on a cosmic liturgy ("The Mass on the World"), in which the world itself is transubstantiated by the spirit of Christ's creative energy. One must think that Teilhard, unable to say Mass in the desert, caught up in the vast endlessness of the desert, saw things in a larger and more connected context. One gets a sense of the proportions and solitary majesty of the desert experience in the grandeur of Teilhard's language:

> Since once more, My Lord, not now in the forests of Aigne but in the Steppes of Asia, I have neither bread, nor wine, nor altar, I shall rise beyond symbols to the pure majesty of the real, and I shall offer you. I your priest, on the altar of the whole earth, the toil and sorrow of the world . . .
>
> Receive, my Lord, this one whole victim which creation, drawn by your power, offers up to you in this New Dawn. Bread, our toil, is in itself,

I know, no more than a draught that dissolves; but in the heart of this formless mass you have planted an irresistable and sanctifying urge which makes each one of us, from the godless man to the man of faith, cry out "Lord, make us to be one!"[16]

This sense of vastness in Christ—vastness being one characteristic of desert spirituality—was contrasted in Teilhard's life by that other characteristic of the desert: the sense of one's own personal insignificance before God. It is a clear variation on the theme once enunciated by another great dweller of the desert, John the Baptist: "He must increase, I must decrease" (John 3:30). In an extraordinary letter of 1929, Teilhard took up this idea:

> The longer I live, the more I feel that true repose consists in renouncing one's own self, by which I mean making up one's mind to admit that there is no importance whatever in being "happy" or "unhappy" in the usual meaning of the word. Personal success or personal satisfaction are not worth another thought if one does achieve them, or worth worrying about if they evade one or are slow in coming. All that is really worthwhile is action—faithful action for the world, for God. . . . I have told you more than once that my life is now possessed by this "disinterest" which I feel to be growing on me, while at the same time the deep-seated appetite, that calls me to all that is real at the heart of the real, continues to grow stronger.[17]

Teilhard's meditations and reflections took place amid the life of a busy explorer and scientist. As the quote so eloquently indicates, his mystical vision was not merely an exercise in satisfying the self, Teilhard wanted to live a life of "faithful action for the world, for God"; and it is against that desire that his idea of "disinterest" must be understood.

It is a facile stereotype to cast the desert solitary as a solipsist or as possessing something of the narcissistic about himself—"seeking for personal perfection." Yet it is clear that Teilhard envisioned his mystical vision as a way to reinvigorate Christianity. He was painfully aware, as a scientist with full access to the scientific world, that there was a chasm between the world of theology and that of science (all the more acute in his own day when the antimodernist reaction was in full fervor). He was even more conscious of the terrible powers that were loose in modern culture. In 1940, Teilhard was in Peking; the Vichy government ruled over large portions of his homeland; and he was only intermittently in contact with Europe. From Peking, he could see, telescopically, as it were, the clouds of war rolling over the face of Europe. He would soon experience some of the privations of war in the East. It was from this vantage point of isolation and distance that he could see the urgency of a new way of looking at the world. He saw the time as an opportunity, perhaps the final opportunity, for Christianity:

> Christianity must show itself, with all its resources for renewal, now or never: God, the Christ, presenting Himself as the focus of salvation —not simply individual and "supernatural" salvation, but collective and earth embracing too; a new concept, consequently, or charity (incorporating and preserving the sense of the earth); and all this summed up and made concrete in the figure of the universal Christ. I see no other issue to the problems and aspirations of the moment, and I shall never tire of saying or trying to say so. An odd situation; on all sides the battles raged unchecked; but the closer you look at it, if you get back to the source of the conflict, the more clearly you realize that the root of the evil is not in the apparent conflicts but very far away from them, it seems, in the inner fact that men have despaired of God's personality.[18]

When one compares the lives of these two remarkable French desert solitaries, Teilhard and de Foucauld, it is easy to view them as wildly different personalities. Even their superficial similarities (both were passionately religious French aristocrats with a scientific bent of mind) pale against the divergences in their style of life. Yet in the final analysis, their basic vision was not all that distinct. If the desire of de Foucauld was to see Christ *au coeur des masses* (to borrow from a book title of Rene Voillaume, the head of the Little Brothers), one must remember that Teilhard went only a step further, for, it must be remembered, he once wrote a work entitled *Au Coeur de la Matiere*. Both insights came from their stark realization of the hidden, but palpable, presence of God in the world—a presence both men sensed in the absence, silence, violence, and sterility of the deserts of culture and nature.

De Foucauld's followers have interpreted the desert in manmade terms: the desert as a product of human migration, industrial excess, human poverty, and bureaucratic negligence. It is an insight they share with many others who have sensed the same sterility in much of modern culture. It is not without significance that the seminal modernist poem of the English-speaking world in our century is T. S. Eliot's "The Waste Land." Again one thinks of the experience of the late Simone Weil. In the 1930s, still very much the searcher and as yet untouched by the graces of mystical prayer, she voluntarily worked in the factories of France as a way of overcoming the gap between her philosophical bent and her instinct for the masses of workers in France. In essays like "Factory Work," Weil sketches out the essentially alienating element in industrial labor as she perceived it through her own experiences. It is the machine, not the operator of the machine, that is at home in the factory. The machine is served by the worker and not vice versa. The wretched haste of piecework is bereft of contemplative dignity or creativity: "It comes natural to a man, and it befits him, to pause having finished something, if only for an instant, in order to contemplate his handiwork, as God did in Genesis. Those lightening moments of thought, of immobility and equilibrium, one has to learn to eliminate utterly in a workday at a factory."[19]

One aspect of the desert, then, is its sterility and its lifelessness. The followers of Charles de Foucauld see the modern desert as being urban, not rural; manmade, not natural; dense, not scattered. They respond to this new desert by trying to insert a religious presence as a paradoxical sign that (again, to paraphrase a book title from Bishop Helder Camara) the desert is fertile.

By contrast, the desert for Teilhard de Chardin was seen in a much more optimistic light. The desert was simply desert, a phenomenon of nature, a harshly beautiful, silent landscape that creates for those who enter it the context for a deeper sense of God's presence in the world.

The desert component of Teilhard's spirituality was a ringing affirmation of the goodness of this world. Even in the harshly bleak solitudes of China or Mongolia, Teilhard affirmed the judgment of the Book of Genesis: "God saw all things that He had made, and they

were very good" (Gen. 1:31). This foundational faith in the goodness
of the world is nowhere better expressed than in the extraordinary
meditation on Elijah and the fiery chariot that Teilhard appended to
the end of *The Heart of Matter*. This "hymn to matter" begins with
a line that evokes *The Canticle* of Saint Francis and the austerity of
the desert solitary: "Blessed be you, harsh matter, barren soil, stub-
born rock: You who yield only to violence, you who force us to work
if we would eat." The hymn ends with these lines as Elijah is swept
up in fire to God: "Raise me up then, matter, to those heights,
through struggle and separation and death; raise me up until, at long
last, it becomes possible for me in perfect chastity to embrace the
universe. Down below on the desert sands, now tranquil again, someone was weeping and calling out: 'My father, my father! What wild
wind can this be that has borne him away?' And on the ground there
lay a cloak."[20]

Teilhard's view of the desert was a positive one. In that, he was
not unlike the late Thomas Merton, who viewed the desert and the
wilderness as a positive environment set out by God for contemplative good. There was a persistent streak of antiurbanism in Merton.
It is not surprising then that Merton could argue that part of the
monk's obligation was to create and maintain the desert wilderness
for the sake of others who would need an alternative to the city:
"Surely there are enough people in the cities already without monks
adding to their number when they would seem to be destined by
God, in our time, to be dwellers in the wilderness and also its protec-
tors."[21]

However differently Charles de Foucauld, Thomas Merton, or
Teilhard de Chardin conceived of the desert, they did have this one
thing in common: They went to the desert willingly. In this, they
share a common heritage with the whole desert tradition of biblical
and postbiblical culture. The desert, in short, was a choice. In our
times, however, there is a phenomenon, if not peculiar to, certainly
characteristic of, modernity: the creations of deserts to which people
are driven.

In another place, I have argued that Elie Wiesel's poignant memoir of the Nazi death camps *(Night)* was an inversion of the Exodus

story in the Bible.[22] By that I meant that Wiesel told the story of his youth as a Jew in Eastern Europe and later in Auschwitz by, consciously or unconsciously, using the language of the Exodus account of the Jews leaving Egypt for the desert. The Jewish people were "called out by the Nazis"; an insane woman dreamed, by night, of fire and the victims saw the smoke of the camps by day. Their place of living was absolutely sterile and without life. They went to that place, not to find God, but to lose Him. The manna of Auschwitz was grudgingly given bread and soup that tasted of corpses. The divine process of "election" now became the dreaded act of "selection"—the languidly pointed finger of Doctor Josef Mengeles that sentenced a person to the gas chambers.

Wiesel is one of the many who have written of the "going out" into the desert of the Nazi camps (how many there are who have left no record of the Exodus) just as a flood of memoirs is now appearing about that other great desert of our time: the Gulag. Solzhenitsyn and Mandelstam have recorded the physical desert of the Gulag while others, like Vladimir Bukovsky, have testified to the latest desert of the modern totalitarian state: the punitive psychiatric hospital.

There is no possibility of discussing these "nay sayers" in any extended way. What is important to note, however, is that all of them reflect an absolute imperative to rise above—to transcend, if you will —a temptation to the fatalism such absolutely destructive environments generate. For Wiesel, and others like him, it is the sacred duty of the survivor not to let the world forget, even if the world is tired of listening or irritated at being reminded of what happened in the great evil deserts of our time. "Let us tell tales," Wiesel has written, "so as to remember how vulnerable man is when faced with overwhelming evil. Let us tell tales so as not to give the executioner the last word. The last word belongs to the victim. It is up to the witness to capture it, shape it, transmit it and keep it as a secret, and then communicate the secret to others."[23]

Similarly, Aleksandr Solzhenitsyn conceives of his task in explicitly religious terms, terms that have not endeared him to everyone in Western society because of the stern and unbending moral tone. Leonard Shapiro, in an essay on Solzhenitsyn's *Gulag*, characterizes his witness not so much in terms of martyrdom (that is, witnessing for truth) but "far nearer to the traditional Orthodox idea of *podvizh-nichestvo*, the valiant and open performance of acts of faith for the glory of the Faith."[24]

The twentieth-century version of the lives of the Desert Fathers may not be coming (indeed, for the most part, are not coming) from the monasteries, charterhouses, and Carmels of organized Christianity as much as from the prisons, the camps, the psychiatric hospitals, and the detention centers of totalitarian centers both in the East and the West. Today we read the ancient *Verba Seniorum* ("The Sayings of the Desert Fathers") with a certain diffidence.[25] They represent a time long ago, a culture now past, and a world view essentially alien to our own. But we read such sayings nonetheless. They represent a tradition that has its own attractiveness: They are spare and stripped to essentials. Their very terseness attracts as does the Zen koan or the Sufi wisdom story. They reflect a wisdom in contact with perennial issues: mastery of the self, growth in love, perseverance, the desire for fullness, the reality of evil.

That tradition has not died in our own time. Millions are nourished by the writings of the spiritual masters who have voluntarily sought the desert. Yet, beyond their witness is the testimony of those who have been sent to the desert. It is a desert that is as real and as alien as the ancient Thebiad. It is the desert of authentic evil and the shadow of death lies over it. It presents the same problem as the ancient deserts: How does one remain human in the face of all that is lifeless and inhuman? The new fathers of the desert are numerous; they are as well known as Bonhoeffer, Wiesel, and Solzhenitsyn and as hidden and obscure as the unnumbered persons who smuggle letters and protests from jails in Latin America, Russia, and the Far East.

The voices coming to us from the "new deserts" are not always explicitly religious or openly spiritual. Not every political dissident is a saint, but neither was every monk who fled to the desert in the fourth century. We can only expect that the desert will produce a saint appropriate to that milieu. It will be from these saints that we will have stories and exemplary lives to aid us in these times of extreme circumstance. Nearly a generation ago the world became aware of one of the first of the really famous Russian dissidents when the Soviet Union forbade Boris Pasternak to accept the Nobel Prize for literature awarded to him in 1958. After that event, Thomas Merton wrote some lines about Pasternak that could stand as a shorthand description for the kind of sanctity we should expect from the manmade deserts of our world:

> His "religious" character is something more general, more mysterious, more existential. He has made his mark in the world not so much by what he said as by what he was: the sign of a genuinely spiritual man. . . . He embodied in himself so many of the things modern man pathetically claims he still believes in, or wants to believe in. He became a kind of "sign" of that honesty, integrity, sincerity, which we tend to associate with the free and creative personality. . . . In one word, Pasternak emerged as a genuine human being stranded in a mad world. He immediately became a symbol, and all those who felt it important not to be mad attached themselves in some way to him.[26]

From the wrestlings of these new hermits in the desert, we gain a new insight into ancient spiritual problems. We are learning that the *noche oscura* of the mystics is not merely desolation in prayer and dryness in faith; it is a blocked horizon where no human hope seems to appear; after all, did not Elie Wiesel call Auschwitz the "Kingdom of Night"? The demonic forces of the old hagiography were seen as fearsome beasts or seductive phantasms. When the new Boschs and Dalis come to illustrate again the temptations of our Saint Anthonys, the iconography will not be gleaned from ancient bestiaries; it will be an iconography of jackboots, advanced chemical gases, instruments to shock, mind-altering drugs, and bureaucratic regimentations. It is a hagiography that is available at the corner drugstore. We ignore its message at our own peril.

NOTES

1. This juxtaposition of texts suggested itself to me as a result of reading William Johnson, *The Inner Eye of Love: Mysticism and Religion* (San Francisco: Harper and Row, 1978), p. 98.

2. James W. McClendon, *Biography as Theology* (Nashville: Abingdon, 1974), p. 92.

3. Herbert Schneidau, *Sacred Discontent: The Bible and the Western Tradition* (Berkeley: University of California Press, 1976), p. 145.

4. Henri Frankfort et al., *Before Philosophy: The Intellectual Adventure of Ancient Man* (Baltimore: Penguin, 1961), p. 246.

5. Schneidau, *Sacred Discontent*, p. 143.

6. Saint Athanasius, "Life of Saint Anthony," trans. Mary Emily Keenan in *Early Christian Biographies*, edited by Roy J. DeFerrari (Washington: Fathers of the Church, 1952), pp. 181–82. On the whole tradition, see "Eremetisme." In *Dictionnaire de Spiritualité*, vol. 4 (Paris: Beauchesne, 1960), pp. 937–982.

7. Chapter 44, Saint Athanasius, *Life of Saint Anthony*, p. 175.

8. Timothy Ware, *The Orthodox Church* (Baltimore: Penguin, 1963), p. 48.

9. Thomas Merton, "Wilderness and Paradise." In Patrick Hart, ed., *Monastic Journey* (Garden City: Doubleday Image, 1978), p. 189. The entire essay is a review of some recent books on the desert motif in the Bible and the subsequent history of Christianity and, as such, is important as background for this chapter.

10. Among the biographies, none totally satisfactory, are Michael Carrouges, *Soldier of the Spirit: The Life of Charles De Foucauld* (New York: Putnam, 1956); Anne Fremantle, *Desert Calling: The Life of Charles De Foucauld* (London: Hollis and Carter, 1950); Margaret Trouncer, *Charles De Foucauld* (London: Harrap, 1972). There is also an adequate survey of his life in Hilda Graef, *Mystics of Our Time* (Paramus: Paulist, 1963), pp. 127–152.

11. The letters from this period have been published: *Inner Search: Letters (1889–1916)* (Maryknoll: Orbis, 1979).

12. Trouncer, *Charles De Faucauld*, p. 138.

13. Besides Carlo Carretto, *Letters From the Desert* (Maryknoll: Orbis, 1972), the same publishers have also published his *The God Who Comes* (1974); *In Search of the Beyond* (1975); *Love is for Living* (1977); *Summoned by Love*. (1979)

14. Paoli's works in English include (from Maryknoll: Orbis) *Freedom To Be Free* and *Meditations on Saint Luke*. Paoli is a frequent contributor to the Florentine journal, *Testimonianze*.

15. Pierre Teilhard de Chardin, *Letters from a Traveller* (New York: Harper and Row, 1962), pp. 85–86. The literature on Teilhard is immense; the following have been useful for me: N. M. Wildiers, *An Introduction to Teilhard de Chardin* (New York: Harper and Row, 1968); Henri de Lubac, *Teilhard de Chardin: The Man and His Meaning* (New York: Mentor Books, 1964); Henri

de Lubac, *The Religion of Teilhard de Chardin* (Garden City: Doubleday Image, 1968); Christopher Mooney, *Teilhard de Chardin and the Mystery of Christ* (Garden City: Doubleday Image, 1969).

16. The full text can be found in Pierre Teilhard de Chardin, *The Heart of Matter*, trans. Rene Hague (New York: Harcourt Brace Jovanovich, 1979), pp. 119–134. The same volume reproduces Teilhard's seminal essay, "The Christic" (pp. 80–102), which deepens this prayer while demonstrating that the "Mass" was central to Teilhard's spiritual vision.

17. Teilhard, *Letters*, p. 160.

18. Ibid., p. 269.

19. The essay can be found in *Cross Currents* (Winter 1976), pp. 367–382. It is also readily available in George Panichas, ed., *The Simone Weil Reader* (New York: McKay, 1977), pp. 53–72.

20. Teilhard, *The Heart of Matter*, pp. 75–76.

21. Hart, *The Monastic Journey*, p. 196.

22. Lawrence S. Cunningham, "Elie Wiesel's Anti-Exodus." In Harry Cargas, ed., *Responses to Elie Wiesel* (New York: Persea Books, 1978), pp. 23–28.

23. Elie Wiesel, "Art and Culture After the Holocaust," *Cross Currents* (Fall 1976), p. 258.

24. Leonard Shapiro, "Disturbing, Fanatical, and Heroic," *The New York Review of Books* (November 13, 1975), p. 15.

25. Compare Thomas Merton, *The Wisdom of the Desert: Sayings from the Desert Fathers of the Fourth Century* (New York: New Directions, 1970).

26. Thomas Merton, *Disputed Questions* (New York: Farrar, Straus, and Giroux, 1960), pp. 4–5.

CHAPTER 6

The Tradition of the Saints: A Reflection

In our search for the new models of sanctity appropriate for our age and condition, we cannot ignore or bypass the great hagiographical tradition of the past. Only the most radically revisionist critics would seriously argue that the tradition of Christian sanctity is without merit or irrelevant to Christian life today. Indeed, as I noted earlier, some of the most creative religious personalities and movements of our time have looked back to the saints of old in order to derive models for their own life story or their own spiritual development. One could argue, for example, that the Catholic Worker Movement here in America is, at base, an attempt to rethink the radical vision of Saint Francis of Assisi. Anyone who is conversant with the writings of Thomas Merton on the relevancy of the contemplative life today will know how deeply he studied the lives of Saints Bruno, Bernard, John of the Cross, and those other contemplative saints who provided the spiritual ancestry of his own style of life. It has been fashionable to single out an activist like Daniel Berrigan as a "new kind of politically active Christian," but he himself points to his Jesuit ancestors (many of them canonized) in Elizabethan England to give his own "outlaw" ministry some historical legitimacy. Mother Teresa, the very personification of the active life, takes as her model Saint Thérèse of Lisieux, a nun of the last century who died as a youth of tuberculosis behind the cloistered walls of a French Carmelite convent.

The historical tradition of the saints is a fertile source of inspiration for the saints of today and for the simple concerned Christian. The problem is that the tradition does not admit of easy entry. There is a dearth of good writing about the saints. It is difficult to think of a really first-rate study of a saint's life *qua* saint's life since the Second Vatican Council. It is not clear whether there are any new Romano Guardinis or Hugo Rahners or Anne Freemantles on the immediate horizon. The traditional lives of the saints—even the best of them —make for difficult reading. Even when we know a good deal about the great Christian figures of the past, they have been badly served by the relative indifference of the theologians and spiritual writers. There is far more interest in showing what Saint Thomas Aquinas held or did not hold about systematic theology than why we call him *Saint* Thomas Aquinas. We surely need to study the teachings of Thomas Aquinas, but we would also benefit from serious attention to his interior religious life. What we know of him as a saintly man is too often limited to the pious legend or some minor *obiter dictum* preserved in the legends about him.

Resistance to a serious consideration of the hagiographical tradition springs, one suspects, from the fact that the provenance of hagiography is thought to be "low-culture" Christian writing. The saints have not seriously engaged the attention of the theological community since the Patristic period; the sorry consequence of that fact has been that much of hagiography has been largely left to the antiquarian, the curious, or the uncritically pious.

The word "hagiography" does not enjoy a positive meaning today. As an adjective, "hagiographical" is used to describe those books (usually biographies) that are exercises in uncritical adulation. To say that a book is hagiographical is to conjure up the image of some work like the campaign biography of an aspiring politician or a piece of self-puffery about a film star "as told to" some professional ghost writer. Such an adjective, in short, characterizes a book that is obsequious, self-serving, and lacking in critical proportion. According to the *Oxford English Dictionary*, hagiography entered the English language with reference to lives of the saints only in the nineteenth century; and its first usage in print was already a pejorative one. Robert Southey, the English critic and poet, used it to describe "Romish hagiography" in 1821; and that seems to have been its first appearance in print in the English language.

It is not difficult to understand how the term hagiography early took on a negative meaning. Even sympathetic scholars like the Bollandist Fathers (who have pioneered hagiographical studies for centuries) recognized that the early lives of the saints were, more often than not, wildly improbable tales replete with excessive violence, extraordinary and extravagant miracles, and curious practices, making little appeal to historical or critical standards of accuracy. This is especially true of those works written before the eighteenth century, when more rigorous standards of historiography began to appear. Furthermore, as I have already noted, there was such indifference on the part of theologians and Church authorities that it was possible (and continues to be possible) to generate and publish the most outlandish material for the supposed edification of the faithful. In fact, some scholars have insisted that in certain areas of the Catholic world, there is a strain of proletarian religion, much of it centered around the cult of the saints, which is only marginally connected with the "official" religion of Catholicism. The Church, it has been said, tolerates this folk religion while recognizing its inherent theological deficiency. It is also interesting that only in more recent times have theologians studied this popular strain of religion. Recently, there has been some focus on the phenomena of this folk religion, especially on the part of those liberation theologians who feel that not enough attention has been paid to religious sentiments that come up "from below" and express the needs and aspirations of the *Lumpenproletariat* of Catholicism, especially in the less-developed areas of the world.[1]

Even the most sophisticated partisans of the saints feel qualms when faced with the polyfaceted phenomena that the lives of the saints present to us. One of the more readable modern books on the saints is the popular work of Phyllis McGinley, *Saint Watching*. A light-hearted reflection on hagiography, it talks about a large number of saints from the historical tradition of Catholicism (well over a hundred saints are mentioned in her text) under various headings, such as "saints and nature" and "women saints". Yet it is interesting (and telling) that when one reads the book carefully, a relatively small number of names keeps coming up again and again: Augustine of Hippo, Bernard of Clairvaux, Francis of Assisi, Catherine of Siena, Joan of Arc, John of the Cross, Teresa of Avila, Jerome, Francis De Sales, and Ignatius Loyola. Were one to go to most of the more recent collections of lives of the saints, those same persons will appear more often than not.

Why should that be? Part of the answer is that those mentioned (and some others like them) have been remembered in the hagiographical tradition as real persons rather than mere symbols. We have some evidence of their person from their own writings or from eyewitness accounts that inform us of the perceptions of others. In the tradition of hagiography, we have so many instances of personages who are semilegendary or about whom we know nothing. They are not people; they are emblems. Others are so shadowy as persons (for example, the early martyrs) that we have no sense of them as human beings. They merely represent an ideal. As such, they take on a role in iconography or symbolism, but they fail to provide us with any sense of how their lives could inform our own. What, for example, are we to make of saints such as Jude, Christopher, George, or Barbara beyond their iconographical presence in the folklore of Christianity?

Furthermore, the saints who manifest some sense of human personality bear witness to a truth I have articulated in an earlier chapter. Saints like Francis of Assisi or Joan of Arc help us to understand new ways of being a Christian or their lives sum up some crucial elements that were peculiar to their era or of an immense value to it. They served a paradigmatic function in the development of Christianity. That is why, in retrospect, we are able to call a certain period the "Age of Saint Augustine" or the "Age of Aquinas"; that is why we can get a better grasp of the spirit of the Counter-Reformation by an intense scrutiny of the life and spiritual doctrine of Saint Teresa of Avila. It is interesting, in this regard, that the saints discussed by

McGinley who lived before the fourteenth century all appeared in Dante's *Paradiso* in some symbolic capacity. Dante used the saints in the *Paradiso* to represent the qualities of the Beatific Vision of the saved and to represent the gifts of divine grace in a special way. Saint Augustine is one of the "Sapienti"; Aquinas is the spokesman for the theologians; Francis of Assisi is a paradigmatic figure of love; and Saint Bernard of Clairvaux is the contemplative intercessor who pleads Dante's case to the Virgin before he can enjoy the vision of God in the final canto of the poem.

Not only have these better remembered saints served as paradigms for certain moments in Christian history, but also, in some cases, they have so captured the imagination that their role has taken on a larger function that goes well beyond any narrow sectarian or religious sentiment. Saint Joan of Arc (1412–1431) has not only been a national symbol of French patriotism and national spirit, but she has also captured the literary imagination of authors as different as Vita Sackville-West and George Bernard Shaw. Her *persona* has been interpreted on the screen by actresses of the stature of Ingrid Bergman and Jean Seberg. Saint Francis of Assisi is "everybody's favorite saint." Any visitor to Assisi can testify to the ecumenical nature of the pilgrimages that come to that Umbrian hill town to commune with his spirit there. Saint Francis has been a central character in the Romantic revival of interest in things medieval that got started in the last century.[2] In the university town where I live, there is both an Episcopal church and a nonprofit league for the care of injured animals under the patronage of his name. Even so unlovely a person as Saint Jerome ("a man with a difficult, cantankerous temperament and a sarcastic wit that made him enemies") served as a paradigmatic figure for a certain age in the Church.[3] The many paintings and drawings of him in the Renaissance period (the engraving of Dürer being the most famous) testify to his popularity with those humanists and philogists who saw in Jerome's life a model for their own: a life of retirement, study, and philological research dedicated to the reform of Church and life. Jerome had the further advantage of having lived prior to the time of scholastic thought, something the humanists heartily despised. It is no wonder that contemporary drawings of Erasmus borrow from the iconography of Jerome to show Erasmus as scholar/reformer. Jerome was a model to emulate.

The saints serve more than a symbolic function to sum up an age or give expression to a historical period. It is possible for a serious scholar or an inspired literary artist to recreate, from the stuff of a saint's life or thought, a rather complete picture of the saint's own time or insights that might aid in the search for spiritual understanding in a later period. While I have spoken in this book somewhat disparagingly of "hagiography," I freely acknowledge that certain studies of the saint have had artistic, spiritual, and intellectual value. I have already noted how the life of Saint Joan of Arc triggered the imagination of playwrights, poets, novelists, and filmmakers. But there have been other examples of this kind of artistic activity in our century. Religious fidelity in the face of official enmity and even death has been amply explored in T. S. Eliot's blank verse drama on the life of Saint Thomas of Becket, *Murder in the Cathedral.* The same theme of religious fidelity is at the heart of Robert Bolt's justly praised *A Man for All Seasons,* which, in turn, was rendered cinematically in an award-winning film by Fred Zinneman. At times, the story of a saint can be transposed into different forms of artistic media without doing essential violence to its authenticity. Thus, Gertrud von Le Fort's novel about the Carmelite martyrs of the French Revolution *(The Song of the Scaffold)* became an able play in the hands of George Bernanos *(The Dialogue of the Carmelites)* which, in turn, was made into a brilliant opera by Poulenc.

Close attention to the life and times of a saint can also yield a deepened picture of that saint's culture when the study is done by a sensitive historian. Iris Origo's brilliant *The World of San Bernardino* (1963) is a splendid evocation of life in the fifteenth century gleaned from a close study of the fiery Franciscan's topical allusions in his preaching. Romano Guardini's *The Conversion of Saint Augustine* (1960) is a penetrating meditation on religious psychology; Peter Brown's *Saint Augustine of Hippo* (1967) uses biography to do intellectual history of the very highest order. That the lives of the saints, even those not generally regarded as first-rate theologians or mystical writers, can provide ample room for creative religious thought is best proved by the example of the towering figure of Baron Von Hügel. His classical work, *The Mystical Element in Religion* (1902), is still valuable; it is, in fact, a detailed study of the rather piously exuberant writings of the Italian mystic, Saint Catherine of Genoa. Sensitive writers like E. Allison Peers or Gerald Brenan, both Hispanists of the first rank, have provided the world with many studies and translations of the great mystics like John of the Cross, Teresa of Avila, and Ignatius Loyola. They combine in their work a highly developed sense of scholarly commitment and an awareness of the value of these saintly persons. They combine in their work a respect for the symbolic value of the saint and an awareness of the saint's power as a symbolic figure.

One should not underestimate the strong symbolic value that a saint can represent for a people or a culture. When, shortly after his elevation to the papacy, Pope John Paul II returned to Poland for the celebration of the nine hundredth anniversary of the martyrdom of Saint Stanislaus, the government was less than pleased, despite Polish pride in the Wojtyla papacy. Saint Stanislaus, after all, was killed because of his unrelenting resistance against a king who acted viciously toward his subjects and who was a persecutor of the Church. The symbolic value of a Catholic bishop who was a saint because he fought the state for its immorality was not lost on the Polish people or on the officially atheistic government, which must live in uneasy peace with the devoutly Catholic presence in Poland. The cult of Saint Stanislaus has a clear political and prophetic edge to it; it constitutes a symbol in the religious order that, despite the murky facts surrounding the actual life and death of Stanislaus, is politically potent and spiritually energizing for the Catholic life of Poland.

Many well-known saints in the Christian calendar are popular despite little being known about them. Their popularity is not based on any discernible moral or spiritual qualities that can be emulated. They have become symbols or talismans for certain ideas, sentiments, or aspirations. Their place of honor is assured because of some function they fulfill in the popular imagination. Until very recently, pious Catholics would have their throats blessed on Saint Blaise's day

(February 3) because that saint (about whom we know practically nothing) is said to have cured a boy once who had a bone stuck in his throat. That story circulated in late lives of the saints and has no historical relationship to the real Blaise if, indeed, there was a Saint Blaise. There was a Saint Patrick; and he did evangelize Ireland from about 435 to his death in 461. But in this country, at least, his considerable historical significance has been downplayed and his symbolical function has been elevated into a sort of jolly nationalism to which a good deal of sentimental Celtic baggage has been appended: the harp, a patriotic parade, the shamrock, and so forth. In a similar manner, Saint Valentine's Day is of far more interest to greeting card and candy makers than to the pious Christian. The correlation between Saint Valentine and lovers is obscure. It is thought to have something to do with his feastday, which is celebrated on February 14. Some scholars trace it to a bit of medieval folklore that says on the fourteenth of February birds chose their mate for spring. Other scholars see it as a carryover from the celebration of the Roman *Lupercalia,* a time thought to be propitious for choosing a marriage partner. The whole situation is all the more confusing because there are two Saint Valentines (one an early Roman martyr buried in Rome and the other a bishop whose remains are venerated in the Italian town of Terni), and it seems that both of them can lay claim to being the Saint Valentine of February 14.[4]

Perhaps the best known saint in America is Santa Claus. Santa Claus (elliptical form of Saint Nicholas) is a redoing of the story of Saint Nicholas, who was venerated in the Low Countries like Holland as the patron of children. Dutch Protestants brought Santa Claus to this country, where his current incarnation is a mixture of the old Catholic patron Saint Nicholas and a legendary magician who rewards good children and punishes evil ones. His feast (December 6) became identified in time with Christmas. The real Saint Nicholas is one of the most venerated saints in the Eastern Church and his cult is one of the most ancient. He appears often in medieval art and in plays of the Middle Ages. There is a highly evolved set of legendary miracle stories about him. It is said that the pawnbroker's symbol of three brass balls echoes a legend of Saint Nicholas, who left bags of gold for three young ladies who needed dowries in order to marry. The *Oxford Dictionary of Saints* lists pictures and stained glass windows of him in places as widely scattered as Istanbul, Venice, Sicily, England, and France, making him, even beyond the Middle Ages, "the most frequently represented saintly bishop for many centuries."[5]

Saint Jude the Apostle (about whom we know nothing except what scanty information we have from the New Testament) is widely venerated as the "patron of hopeless cases"—possibly because his name is so similar to that of Judas the betrayer that he was called on only in the direst of circumstances. Even Saint Anthony of Padua (1195–1231), about whom we do know a good deal, is popularly venerated less for his person and his apostolate and more for his reputation as a miracle worker, with some of the more famous miracles now immortalized in bronze by Donatello at the Padua Basilica of Saint Anthony. Anthony is called upon as the saint who will cause lost things to be found, an association probably based on popular stories that were generated by medieval preachers. Even the miracle stories and "pious incidents" of the saint's life seem to be the result of conflating a number of different lives into one about Saint Anthony.

Another category of saints has only a localized or specialized position in the Church's tradition. Any number of religious orders venerated their founders as saints even though, with the notable exception of such persons as Saint Ignatius Loyola, Saint Benedict, and Saint Teresa of Avila, most are unknown outside their respective religious families. In the post-Tridentine Church, there was a veritable plethora of male and female religious orders founded with a corresponding number of canonized founders who, for most Catholics, remain obscure: John Baptist de la Salle, Anthony Mary Claret, John Leonardi, and Paul of the Cross. Other saints are known only locally and their cult is centered in some geographical place. Any country that has had a long history of Christian presence has a corresponding number of saints that are local to that country and about whom little is known outside of those geographical and/or cultural confines. The long list of Anglo-Saxon or Celtic saints in the

British Isles is a good example of this local tradition.

Just as there are saints who are known only by reason of their geographical locale, so there are others who so reflect the values and limitations of their own time that they seem to us quaint at best and almost pathological at worst. It is an element of hagiography that cannot be ignored even though it causes the most ambivalence for believer and unbeliever alike. It would take a singular person, indeed, to be totally approving of someone like the Peruvian mystic Saint Rose of Lima (1586–1617), who undertook fantastic penances that, in these post-Freudian days, cannot be viewed as anything more than aberrational: Rose scarred her face and laced it with pepper to discourage the glance of men; she dipped her hand in lye after someone spoke of the beauty of her hands; she habitually wore a metal crown of thorns on her head, chains on her body, and penitential garments of haircloth under her clothes.[6] Even if we grant her the cultural limitations of the place and time of her life, we must recognize a somewhat aberrant personality goaded to excess by an admiring populace who saw in her penances a kind of vicarious penance for their own sins and shortcomings. Public adulation (she was widely venerated as a saintly intercessor and miracle worker in her own lifetime) reinforced an exaggerated sense of penance and religious discipline that was endemic in the spirituality of the time. Rose of Lima, of course, goes back in tradition to a stream of asceticism as old as the Desert Fathers (compare the penances of Saint Simon Stylites) and finds its adherents throughout Christian asceticism. Such ascetics have fascinated artists of our own time (compare the fiction of Gustave Flaubert; the autobiographical memoir, *Report to Greco,* by Nikos Kazantzakis; and such films of Louis Buñuel as *San Simeon* and *Nazarin*); but as a rule, these folk merit more admiration (in the old sense of *admiratio,* wonder) than emulation.

What, then, are we to make of this long and byzantine tradition with its fictionalized heroes, its symbolic personages, its semidivinities, its miracle workers, its ascetics, and its authentically fresh personalities? The tendency in the modern Catholic Church is to let the whole tradition of the saints—as they have been traditionally understood—fall into a kind of benign neglect or, what is worse, to trivialize and sentimentalize the tradition into inane consumerism: concrete statues of Saint Francis for the suburban garden or a Saint Christopher medal in anodized, salt-resistant metal for the speedboat. It is true that the canonization procedures go on at their slow pace, but it is equally true that such procedures win less than enthusiastic attention from most Catholics. The Sanctoral cycle of the liturgy is still celebrated, but with an observance that is perfunctory. Nor is there any evidence, as I have already noticed, that theologians are doing much serious reflection on the relevance or even the meaning of the saint in the Christian tradition.

In the face of this neglect and indifference, the remaining part of this chapter will argue that the tradition of the saints in Catholicism should not be left to the trivializers or the credulous. In fact, this chapter will argue that there is much to be learned by a patient reconsideration of the tradition of hagiography. If there is an evident desire today for a new sense of what it means to be a Christian—and there is every indication of an intense interest in such a topic—then some of the lessons of the tradition of the saints may be valuable for us to ponder. This is a vast subject (and a vast challenge), but it may be possible to give some hints that will spur others to more complete considerations of what I merely sketch in at this time.

In the first place, a sustained history of hagiography can offer us some insights into the history and development of Christianity *from below* instead of *from above*. We usually study Christianity from above in the sense that our sources are usually taken from those "official" compilations such as chancery records, conciliar collections, and insight into studies of the Fathers and the theologians. It is true that some hagiography did come "from above" in the sense that the stories of the saints, especially after the Middle Ages, were compiled for the canonization process. Such history from above tends to be rigidly orthodox and self-censoring. It is characteristically focused on what is official, determinative, and influential. It is, *pari passu*, male, clerical, rational, political, and redolent of "high culture." By contrast, much of the tradition about the saints is intermingled with folk tales, popular beliefs, homely iconography, and striking leaps of the imagination and often done with an eye for popular rather than elitist consumption. In that sense, the lives of the saints tell us something about what the compilers wanted the populace to hear and, conversely, what the populace desired to hear. At the superficial level, this amounts to the quasi magical, the extraordinary, and the reassuring. Yet, in the welter of this material, there are echoes of a religiosity that is more substantial though little noticed in the "official" concerns of the hierarchy.

The place and role of women in the development of the Christian tradition is a case in point. While it is true that the hagiographical tradition has been far more democratic in its concern for women than have other Church sources, it is not so obvious to me that the full weight of this tradition has been adequately measured. Saints like Catherine of Siena, Teresa of Avila, Clare of Assisi, and a selected number of other women are mentioned over and over again to "show" the role of women in the Church. Until very recently, not very many persons were looking at the lesser known female saints as they appear in the earlier history of the Church to inquire whether they lived and acted according to the stereotypes we expect of them.[7] Nor is it clear that even the best known of the female saints have been adequately studied in terms of any other than the standard categories we have received "from above." For example, we know that Saint Catherine of Siena (died 1380) wrote letters to the popes in the last years of her life to protest the Avignon captivity of the Church. This is remarked on by all of her biographers from Raymond of Capua (her friend) down to the present day. But this has not led anyone—as far as I can ascertain—to inquire into the prophetic role of Catherine in particular and women in general in the Church. Nor does one hear the "official" sources provide us with the example of Catherine of Siena or other women to encourage such prophetic stances. In fact, it seems obvious that people are going to have to search the hagiographical tradition to show such a prophetic function and then construct a more formalized theological reflection from it. Such a task will more than likely not be taken on from above; examples of past prophetic women and prophetic women today—that is, those from below—will be the ones to demonstrate the validity of such a role in the Church.

Beyond the more intense scrutiny of those more famous women in the tradition of the saints are the clusters of lesser known personalities who are worthy of greater attention. Examples of these women abound in hagiography but have received little serious attention from any but the antiquarian. We know, for example, a great deal about the great Saint Jerome (341–342); but little attention has been paid to the circle of women with whom he associated (and about which association he was roundly criticized) in Rome circa 380–383. They are often studied in conjunction with the life of Jerome, but serious reflection needs to be done on their role and influence in the Roman Church. What was the importance of those pious women under Paula who set up a monastery in Bethlehem to parallel that of Saint Jerome? What was the character of their spiritual life and how did they "fit" together with the overall tenor of Jerome's much noted misogyny? How did they see themselves in relationship to the official Church of the time? These are all questions that deserve serious and widespread discussion.

We have another area of fruitful inquiry in areas like the Anglo-Saxon Church. Hilda of Whitby (614–680), whose life and deeds are remembered in Bede's *Ecclesiastical History,* was an extraordinary woman who played a full role in the English Church of the time. She ruled over a monastery of men and women at Whitby. She was the patroness of the poet Caedmon. It was under her guidance that the Synod of Whitby was held, a synod that did much to bring Roman custom to the Anglo-Saxon Church. We know she played a significant role in education since it was under her tutelage that a number of the most important bishops of the time were educated. We need to know, in some detail, whether Hilda was the exception rather than the rule. We need to inquire further how her own society understood her role in the Church and what elements in Christianity make it difficult for us, so many centuries later, to imagine women in such powerful and influential roles in any national church of Catholicism.

When we read of twelfth-century women like Hildegard of Bingen (1098–1179), we find a woman who was not only a mystic (an area in which she has received recognition) but also a writer and artist whose talents produced illustrated works; commentaries on Holy

Scripture; treatises on theology, medicine, natural history, and botany; poetry; and at least one play. This much is well known (although, characteristically enough, she is not mentioned in the indices of such standard works as Gordon Leff's *Medieval Thought: Augustine to Ockham* or David Knowles's *The Evolution of Medieval Thought*), but one must ask why there has been so little attention paid to a woman whose fame "even in the twelfth century spread far outside Germany, to reach Iceland and England"?[8] Furthermore, the life of Hildegard raises many questions that should alter our normal understanding of the Middle Ages: Where did she get her education? To what extent was she an exception rather than the rule in her age? How seriously should we take her claim that the times in which she lived should be considered the "age of the woman" *(tempus muliebre)*, given the weakness of men in the Church? We now know that women were educated and were teachers in the Middle Ages. Dom Jean Leclercq has recently written about the teaching role of women.[9] It is an appropriate time to press these studies if we are to have a clearer understanding of the long-undervalued role of women in the golden period of ecclesiastical learning. A better understanding of that issue should prove fruitful for some of the problems of our own time.

Hagiography provides us not only with a resource for a better understanding of an underdeveloped area such as feminine roles in the Church but it also provides clues for our understanding of other present areas of concern. It is not simply enough to say, for example, that women played a far more significant role in the Church in the past than is generally assumed from our study of Church history from above. There is also an obligation to see if there are moments in the Church's past that might serve us for an understanding of the present. As I have already noted in Chapter 3, the saint should be considered a paradigmatic figure, one who shows us a new or compelling way to be a Christian. The paradigmatic witness of the saint helps us, in turn, to see that there are new possibilities for us. For example, to go back to the life of Saint Catherine of Siena is to see someone whose sanctity and moral authority was such that she could call the papacy back to a sense of its moral obligation. But there is also a further lesson to note in Catherine's activities. It may seem obvious to us now, but it was certainly novel in Christian discourse fifteen years ago: Apart from the teaching authority of the Magisterium, there also exists the moral and spiritual authority of the prophetic charism. In fact, what we learn from the lives of the saints, in many instances, is a form of protest coming up from below to call the Church back to its mission and its integrity. At times, this prophetic gesture can be a negative or symbolic one (for example, Saint Celestine V resigning the papacy for fear of his soul) or that of the exemplary prophet whose life is an indictment of the state of the Church at a given period in history (for example, the evangelical witness of Saint Francis of Assisi coming precisely at the period when papal power was at its apex) or it may be as aggressive and demanding as the public activities of a Saint Bernard of Clairvaux in the twelfth century.

At other times, the saints demonstrate, by indirection to be sure, that a new sense of consciousness is entering the Church. Let me cite an example, again from the history of female saints. Saint Louise de Marillac (1591–1660) was, with Saint Vincent de Paul (1581–1660), the founder of the Sisters of Charity. That foundation demonstrated that nuns did not have to live in a cloister. The insight and discovery of Louise and Vincent was that a distinction could be made between contemplative nuns and sisters who would work for the good of the needy. The first group of French sisters took their vows in 1642 and began their work in the world. While it is common for religious women to work in schools and hospitals today, it was a revolutionary idea in the seventeenth century. It represented a horizon shift in understanding about the roles of women in the active ministry of the Church. Of them, Saint Vincent said, "Your convent will be the house of the sick; your cell a hired room; your chapel the parish church; your cloister the city streets or the hospital wards; your enclosure obedience; your veil modesty."[10]

We must not underestimate how difficult and novel an idea that band of sisters was for the Parisians of the day to accept. Louise was unable to recruit aristocratic ladies to the cause because of the strictures of society. Many people thought the whole idea was indecorous and not fitting for women. But it happened and not only became tolerated, but the Sisters of Charity became almost synonymous with the works of charity in France and elsewhere for the next three centuries. The inference from this moment in hagiography is clear: Things will happen when there are persons with the vision to make them happen. What was conceptualized and carried out in the time of Louise de Marillac was needed for that age. There is no reason to doubt that other persons may show us "this way" or "that way" for ours.

When one looks back through the hagiographical tradition, it becomes evident that some of the saints have lived the fullest possible spiritual life available in their own time and place while others seem to push forward to new and diverse ways of being Christian. Not only has that been true in the past, but it is true in the present. We have seen in our own day persons who have been the very best that a certain kind of Christianity can produce, while there seem to be others who are straining for a new kind of witness that points to a new understanding.

None, we would assume, would deny the immense character and luminous quality of the lives of such persons as the late Pope John XXIII, Mother Teresa of Calcutta, or the American activist, Dorothy Day. When one examines closely their spirituality, it becomes clear that they represent a grasp of the Church and its message that is very traditional. What they all share is an absolutely serene faith in the confines of the Church and a persistent desire to apply the imperatives of the Gospel to their own lives for the good of others. In the case of Mother Teresa, there is the added fact that she seems totally oblivious to the imperatives of history or the realities of politics or ideology. She and her sisters care for the sickest and poorest people in the slums of Calcutta and other cities (including Rome!) simply because there are people in those places who are in need. One doubts whether her style of ministry would be changed were she in Bogota, Moscow, or Peiping. There are the poor and they need to be helped. Period. She clearly stands in a long tradition of saintliness. One thinks, for example, of Saint Peter Claver (1580–1654), who spent forty years in the port city of Cartagena caring for the slaves in the holds of the slave ships docked there. His concern was not for the abolition of slavery but for the simple task of alleviating suffering where he found it. It could be argued that, in the long run, the religious and social reformers who fought for the abolition of the slave trade were far more important in the eradication of the problem of slavery. That is undoubtedly true. The point is, however, that Peter Claver saw no way to do that given his own position and time. What he did, he did as best he could. There was pain and he tried to do something about it. Arnold Lunn caught this idea rather well (even if a bit unfairly): "The modern social reformers, had they been translated in time to Cartagena, would have sympathized with the Negro slaves, and might have devised admirable schemes for educating them and raising their social status. They would have found it far less easy to simulate affection for them as individuals. You see, in the first place, they stank in those holds of the slave ships and it is so very difficult to love people who stink."[11]

What Lunn captured in that somewhat condescending passage is an approach to saintliness that is very traditional in the Church. It is the notion that the acts of the saints are somehow detached from the social structures or historical exigencies of the time. The need for prayer and/or service is the same today as it was a thousand years ago. The saint, as it were, transcends the limits of this historical situation by doing that which is saintly. Thus, Mother Teresa of Calcutta is totally indifferent to planning policy, political schemes, development programs, or the conventional wisdom about how social problems are to be solved. Her vocation is to take care of the destitute dying until such social policies work. Her work is in the arena of immediate need. It may have a profound impact on our history, but it is essentially an ahistorical exercise. It can be done any time and in any place.

The great saints of charity, whether it be a Martin of Tours, who divided his cloak with a beggar fifteen hundred years ago, or an unnamed Catholic Worker who endures the violent squalor in one of our contemporary cities, does exactly the same thing: service to others in the name of Christ and after the manner of Christ. Such saints are not merely overly developed social workers; such a view is sentimental and anachronistic. The entire history of Christian sanctity demonstrates over and over again that the great saints (and the millions about whom we know nothing) persisted in their lives of charity because of their prior religious conversion. Voltaire, no friend of organized religion, once remarked that Saint Vincent de Paul (died 1660) was a favorite of his because he was the "saint of human misery." Henri Bremond, however, was closer to the mark when he wrote that Vincent de Paul was not a saint because of his charity; he was charitable because he was a saint. Activities like those of Vincent de Paul require only a radical conversion of life, which then compels the person to act out the consequences of that conversion. The charitable or intellectual or spiritual activities might take different forms in different circumstances, but such intense sanctity is always characterized by that same basic impulse: total self giving after the imitation of Christ.

Perhaps the clearest modern theoretical formulation of the timeless character of sanctity is to be found in T. S. Eliot's *Four Quartets*. The quartets (like the complex late quartets of Beethoven) are an extremely dense meditation on the problem of the passage of time and the possibility of human meaning in the flux of time. Eliot, a devout Christian, sees the Incarnation as the supreme moment when the fragility of time intersects with the Infinite. For Eliot, it is difficult for the average person to experience the timeless moment in one's human life. There are moments (Eliot describes one in the "Rose Garden Experience," which begins *Burnt Norton*, the first of the quartets) when we describe the fleeting sense of the Infinite. Only the saint has a continuous sense of the presence of the Infinite in the midst of the real passage of time in life. Eliot writes,

> to apprehend
> The point of intersection of the timeless
> With time, is an occupation for the saint—
> No occupation either, but something given
> And taken, in a lifetime's death in love,
> Ardour and selflessness and self-surrender.
> For most of us, there is only the unattended
> Moment, the moment in and out of time,
> The distraction fit, lost in a shaft of sunlight,

The wild thyme unseen, or the Winter lightening
Or the waterfall, or music heard so deeply
That it is not heard at all, but you are the music
While the music lasts. These are only hints and guesses,
Hints followed by guesses; and the rest
Is prayer, observance, discipline, thought and action.
The hint half guessed, the gift half understood, is
      Incarnation.

("DRY SALVAGES" in *Four Quartets*)

Eliot's saint, as Derek Traversi has pointed out, is the one who can best sustain the level of awareness of the Infinite in the pressure of the finite because, in giving more (the life of heroic virtue), the saint has received more (the heroic state of sanctity—given by grace).[12] To that degree, the saint is a benchmark for the fleeting moments in which, not saints by that understanding, we receive some understanding of the sense of the Infinite, which is God.

It should be noted here (and I have pressed this point a bit earlier in the chapter) that such an understanding of the saint is somewhat ahistorical in character. In Eliot's view of things, it is the overcoming of history by the intersection of the Infinite that is the goal of the saint. The point is worth noting because it may also help us to understand some of the current diffidence toward the character of saintliness in our time.

There is a sense today (most evident in some of the liberation theologians) that genuine sanctity and religious faith cannot transcend the flow of history or stand back from it. There is more of a sense of the exigencies of the here and now. If we are to see saints today, this argument runs, it must be a sanctity that is fully committed to this historical time and this particular place. It does make a difference, these theologians would insist, what the government is, what its policies are, how people perceive their place in life, and what the current struggles and needs demand. Others, less enamored of liberation themes, see the need in terms of a new understanding of what religious symbolism is for our time. Andrew Greeley, for example, wants us to reflect on a "new agenda" in which the perennial values of religious symbol systems are to be understood within the changed historical system in which we find ourselves. It would be interesting to speculate on what a saint of the new agenda would look like. Greeley offers us no candidates, but he or she would have to transcend the historical limitations of the old agenda, which Greeley sees as passing away in Catholic Christianity.[13]

To this point in my inquiry, I have been reflecting on the tradition of hagiography in order to argue that such a tradition may help us understand some past currents of Catholicism from below in order to get a more balanced view of Christianity and to note, in passing, the inherent possibilities for change reflected in the hagiographical tradition. There is one more aspect of hagiography that I would like to think about in the remaining part of this chapter. A good deal of traditional hagiography is pure fiction. It is the fictional character of hagiography that demands some reflection since, one assumes, a large number of people ignore hagiography because it is "made up" and, beyond that, it is "made up" by pious imaginations that are so extravagant and so removed from our own cultural horizon that it is beyond our serious interest. It is true that a good deal of hagiography is historically preposterous, but it is likewise true that the fictional character of hagiography may offer us a clue for the spirituality of our own age.

Hagiography provides us with a link to the world of the common folk of our Christian past. Hagiography (to be understood in that broad sense that encompasses popular art, legends, writings, memories, and such) served a variety of purposes that are not dissimilar to the purposes of much of popular culture today. The hagiographical tradition was meant to edify the faithful who were exposed to its message. Various hagiographical productions (like a legend or a *translatio*) were meant to persuade an audience of the superiority of the miraculous powers of this or that particular saint. The ability to be persuasive in this regard could have an impact, social and economic, on the well-being of a given monastery, shrine, or town.[14] It is a commonplace of medieval history that relics often formed the centerpiece of a vast outpouring of energy that derived from civic pride and resulted in social well-being. One need only remember the vast importance of such centers of pilgrimage as Campostella, Canterbury, Rome, Chartres, and, of course, the Holy Land.

The imaginative embroidery that went into the written examples

of hagiography was, more often than not, unbridled in its attempt to
outdo other miracle stories in order to enhance the prestige of one's
favorite saint. Much of this material is better left to the attention of
the antiquarian or the scholar of hagiography. At times, however,
hagiography could create something of lasting literary beauty that
would persist in the collective memory of culture. The *Little Flowers
of Saint Francis,* rooted in historical fact but heavily overladen with
fiction and polemic, is a case in point. The *Fioretti* stands as an
extremely pure example of early Italian prose, that has enjoyed a long
devotional life and is still translated, read, and admired today. Indeed,
I remember with intense pleasure a theatrical production of some of
its stories performed on a summer evening before the facade of the
lovely Romanesque Church of San Miniato al Monte in Florence by
the *Piccolo Teatro di Milano* just a few years ago.

The obvious question to ask in this connection concerns the
persistence of the hagiographical tradition in our own time. Lives of
the saints (even those written by recognized scholars) seem to be in
a state of serious decline. While certain small denominational houses
still cater to a small market for such productions, it is not an area of
publishing that attracts much attention. If traditional hagiography is
in decline, the practice of writing such hagiography has not disap-
peared. The new lives of the saints seem to have moved from a
distinct hagiographical genre into a hidden stream of the larger world
of the fictional. Although it is beyond the scope of this book to argue
that thesis in depth, it does seem plausible to assume that one might
still find lives of the saints coming from the product of the artistic
imagination. If the hagiography of the past was able to derive almost
solely from the mind of its writers, there is no reason to think the
modern imagination has abandoned such an enterprise. Indeed, the
thesis being advanced here is that for our time, the world of the
fictional and the imaginative is the place to look for our modern
saints. The case of film may serve as an illustration.

Neil Hurley has recently argued that there are a number of "laws"
that help make film a medium capable of creating intercultural and
interfaith bonds among peoples of the world. Two of these laws are
important for our understanding of paradigmatic figures, namely, the
anthropological law: "people have curiosity about other people and

want to know how they meet the four essential 'whats' of life: a) survival and development, b) love and hate, c) authority and disobedience, and d) ideological systems"; and the *religious law:* people will identify negatively with forms of evil and villainy and positively with sacrifice, suffering, and selfless forms of love."[15]

Films depict a ceaseless stream of heroes, antiheroes, villains, characters, and other "types" of fictional persons. Like much of hagiography, these productions are spurred on by economic, ideological, aesthetic, and social reasons. Again like hagiography, the tradition of the film generates, every now and again, a *persona* who becomes a bit more than a "type" or a "character" or even a "hero." That rare person becomes a powerful paradigm for human living at such a level of sensitivity that sanctity would not be an inappropriate term to describe his or her character.

Neil Hurley characterizes Charlie Chaplin's fictional *persona,* the little tramp, as such a figure. He does not hesitate to call the little tramp a saint. The little tramp has an international symbolic presence (he is known, variously, as Carlito, Charlot, Kärlchen, Carlos, and Carlino) that goes well beyond mere popularity and acceptance. Hurley writes,

> Chaplin is the patron saint of the road. In being alone with him, we feel something archaic, something fundamental; we are not alone, we are free. Chaplin is not anti-social nor asocial; he unites sociability with privacy. . . . The eternal pilgrim, Chaplin's journey down the open road is a call to utopian thinking, to letting fall all those things we cherish and mistakingly think we cannot live without. . . . Charlie, the "little tramp" has been for those who live lives of quiet desperation a "pillar of fire" —whether in the darkness of a subculture of poverty and underdevelopment or of a consumeristic society with compulsive technological rhythms of life. For Chaplin liberation is not verbal; it is not preachment. It means activating alternatives and giving witness by lifestyle.[16]

The point urged here is that if traditional Christian hagiography is such an area of cultural dissonance that we cannot approach it, it may well be that we should turn our attention to analogous genres. Critical attention to the new sources of culture from the perspective of spirituality may be one way to maintain the link with the hagiographical tradition of the past ages of the Church. It may be that in the new cultural manifestations of our age—in the film, in novels, and, yes, even on television—we will find the new paradigmatic figures who will teach us, often by indirection, to be sure, how to enflesh the Gospel in our time.

This suggestion is not as eccentric as it may appear at first glance. A close look at the culture of our time will show that many serious folk, in fact, have explored the world of the fictional for paradigmatic figures of sanctity. Those characters were meant merely to be representative, not exclusive. The history of literature shows us many examples of fictional saints and their subsequent influence in the development of spirituality. Fyodor Dostoevsky thought that Cervantes's Don Quixote was the most Christ-like and totally good person in Western literature. He hoped to draw such characters of his own. From that inspiration, Dostoevsky created literary characters —one thinks immediately of Prince Myshkin, Father Zosima, and Aloysha Karamazov—who have been held up as worthy of inspiration and emulation. The Dostoevskyean characters have been admired and commented on by theologians like Romano Guardini and social activists like Dorothy Day. The fictional characters of the late Albert Camus (especially Doctor Rieux of *The Plague*) have been very much admired as "secular saints" appropriate for the needs of our time. Herman Melville's Billy Budd, a Christ-like martyr, has been set before us again in the haunting opera of Benjamin Britten. The unnamed priest of the *Diary of a Country Priest* by George Bernanos has been a powerful image of faith since the time of its publication.

The above examples could be multiplied, but the point is clear. The imagination can create characters so real and compelling that they can offer clear lessons in the way we should or could live our lives. The Don Quixotes, Billy Budds, and Father Zosimas (like Saint Francis or Saint Teresa) give us the encouragement to be more self-giving, more loving, less inclined to hate, more compelled to love. They invite us, in short, to transcend ourselves.

That is why they are saints.

NOTES

1. The literature on popular religion is vast; recently, the journal *Vita Monastica* (March 1978) published a special issue on popular religion and liturgy. In that issue, one may find a selected bibliography (of about two hundred items) on popular religion.

2. I have tried to outline the Romantic revival of Franciscanism in the last century in Lawrence S. Cunningham, *Saint Francis of Assisi* (Boston: Twayne, 1976).

3. See "Saint Jerome." In David Hugh Farmer, comp. and ed., *Oxford Dictionary of Saints* (Oxford: Clarendon Press, 1978). This new book is a handy volume with good bibliographies of all the saints who are venerated in the British Isles. I have made good use of it in this chapter; it is hereafter cited as *ODS*. For a fuller life of Saint Jerome, see J. N. D. Kelly, *Saint Jerome* (New York: Harper and Row, 1977).

4. On these saints, see *ODS*, under their names.

5. On the Saint Nicholas legend, see Charles W. Jones, *Saint Nicholas of Myra, Bari, and Manhatten: Biography of a Legend* (Chicago: University of Chicago Press, 1978).

6. See *ODS*.

7. One hopeful sign that this situation is changing is the increasing number of papers being presented at national meetings of organizations like the American Academy of Religion. Such papers augur well for sustained publication in this area.

8. Friedrich Heer, *The Medieval World* (New York: Mentor Books, 1978), p. 320.

9. Jean Leclercq, Preface, *Julian of Norwich: Showings* (New York: Paulist, 1978).

10. See *ODS*.

11. Arnold Lunn, *A Saint in the Slave Trade* (London: Sheed and Ward, 1947), p. 23.

12. Derek Traversi, *T. S. Eliot: The Longer Poems* (New York: Harcourt Brace Jovanovich, 1976), p. 178.

13. One must also beware of the limitations of the historical moment; early in the 1960s, Greeley thought that President John Kennedy should be named a "Doctor of the Church" (in his 1967 book, *The Catholic Experience*). The fifty-year rule of the canonization process seems very wise when one reads such suggestions.

14. Patrick Geary, *Furta Sacra: Theft of Relics in the Central Middle Ages* (Princeton: Princeton University Press, 1978), demonstrates how economically important the relic trade was in the early Middle Ages.

15. Neil Hurley, *Theology Through Film* (New York: Harper and Row, 1970), p. 6.

16. Neil Hurley, *The Reel Revolution* (Maryknoll: Orbis, 1978), pp. 104–105.

Epilogue

ONE OF the basic contentions of this book is that no formal canonization process can adequately define who or what the saint is. Those upon whom we confer that title often merit it because of some informal consensus. We sense that certain persons make religious values credible or show us new and creative ways of living out religious values that we affirm intellectually but find hard to incarnate in life gestures. In the case of certain persons, it is quite easy to make the judgment about their saintliness. A Pope John XXIII was so transparently good and holy that even those who were outside the confines of the believing community could sense his saintliness. We must ask, however, whether there are any criteria beyond an intuitive sense that help us to recognize the saint. That question gives rise to a further one—of what value is the saint's life for others?

In an earlier part of this study, I touched on a number of characteristics of saintliness. William James, for example, underscored the close link between the saintly personality and asceticism. James did warn that saintliness and denial of the self had to be kept in some kind of creative tension to avoid asceticism becoming an end rather than a means. Even the most orthodox writers on ascetical theology have recognized the thin line between saintliness and psychological pathology. Asceticism, at base, demands an absolutely ruthless ability to assess accurately the self and rein in the voracious demands of the ego. To resist the ego permits the saintly soul to go out to others and, ultimately, the Other. "To be pure in heart," wrote Dag Hammarskjöld in *Markings,* "means, among other things, to have freed yourself from all such half measures: from a tone of voice which places you in the limelight, a furtive acceptance of some desire of the flesh which ignores the desire of the spirit, a self righteous reaction to others in their moment of weakness."[1]

Asceticism is a slippery term because of certain exaggerations in the history of Christian spirituality. I use the term here not to mean mere somatic denial and certainly not any extreme *askesis* with respect to corporeal or sexual needs. Such *askesis* has its own place in spirituality. Asceticism as a hallmark of sanctity, however, is to be measured against the benchmark of Christ's asceticism, which is perfectly symbolized in the cross. In that sense, asceticism is not to overvalue oneself for the sake of self. True Christian asceticism means, in the last analysis, heroic love. Once we have begun to understand asceticism in this more Christian context, we can also conclude that saintliness can never be thought of as purely personal charism; it is, by definition, social; that is, it is for the benefit of others. We can all hope to be saints, but it is a special gift (and a responsive acceptance of the gift) to be a Saint.

There is a further aspect of saintly asceticism that needs some emphasis. The saints show a great sense of persistence or, what is called in more traditionally pious terms, perseverance. It is one thing to feel a flush of youthful altruism and go out to "do good," "save the world," or "aid the disadvantaged." That desire to do good in its various manifestations is often held for the highest motives of benevolence. The act itself provides a certain elevation of self-esteem when the activity is well received or when one sees some positive results as coming from one's efforts. Enthusiasm tends to flag, however, when efforts are rebuffed or results seem scanty or out of proportion to the effort expended. The saint is one who does good without the reinforcement of praise or the vision of good results. Saint Peter Claver went down to the harbor of Cartagena to minister to the slaves in the holds of the trading ships for over thirty years. He never saw the conditions of the slaves bettered nor did his ministrations seem to act as an effectively prophetic judgment on those who controlled the slave trade. Toward the end of his life, he had to be tied to his saddle to make the daily trip to the port since he was too ill to make the trip with his own energies.

It is easy to forget the daily grind of such activities. We read of a Father Damien ministering to the lepers of Molokai or see the photographs of the Catholic Workers on the soup lines of the Lower East Side or view a film of the kindly Doctor Schweitzer moving among his African patients at the hospital at Lambaréné. Such sights move the idealistic. But what is not seen is the sheer drudgery of doing this day in and out, the sheer routine of giving oneself with no end in sight. The saint does such tasks when there is no adulation, no reinforcement of the self, and no consolation.

The ancient ascetics of the desert spoke of the "noonday devil," that spirit of ennui, discouragement, and *accidie* that could afflict the most punctilious of monks. Striking midway through the day (or, as a metaphor, midway through life), after the morning enthusiasm had past and the refreshment of sleep was still hours away, the noonday devil could enervate all efforts of the will. To conquer that temptation, according to the fathers, was to conquer the self. The hallmark of sanctity is the ability to overcome that natural lassitude of the spirit that undermines the day-by-day living out of the radical call to sanctity. The hallmark of the great saint is her precise ability to do just that.

In the contemporary period, the noonday devil has returned to us in the form of boredom (so amply treated by the existentialists) or what Walker Percy has called "everydayness." In his profoundly religious novel, *The Moviegoer,* Percy underscores this everydayness as the underlying problem of contemporary man. His feckless hero, Binx Bolling, lives in a persistent state of oscillation: He seeks out sensory satisfaction while searching for something to assuage permanently his sense of alienation. He was a searcher but he could not always clearly articulate the object of his search. In a passage redolent of Percy's acknowledged master, the Danish theologian, Sören Kierkegaard, Binx muses,

To become aware of the possibility of the search is to be onto something. Not to be onto something is to be in despair.

The movies are onto the search, but they screw it up. The search always ends in despair. They like to show a fellow coming to himself in a strange place—but what does he do? He takes up with the local librarian, sets about proving to the local children what a nice fellow he is, and settles in with a vengeance. In two weeks time he is so stuck in everydayness that he might just as well be dead.[2]

Binx Bolling was not a saint, not even a fictional one like the unnamed curé of George Bernanos. He had, however, put his finger on a crucial element of sanctity: the ability to rise above "everydayness" in a sustained way and in pursuit of a religious vision. For the saint, every moment counts, every effort is intentional, and all action is deliberate. When Saint Francis of Assisi said that because of his conversion he "did not turn away from lepers," he did not become, at that moment, a saint. His sanctity came because it was not a moment but a lifetime of those moments of "not turning away from the lepers," moments that were ever more purified, lucid, and controlled by his prevailing religious commitment.

Heroic sanctity, in other words, is not merely the dramatic moment of intense religious change. I have already noted that sanctity begins in such a conversion; but it does not occur at the precise moment of that conversion. What gives the saint credibility as a saint is the sustained unfolding of his or her life in contact with the ordinary demands of reality. What strikes one about a Dietrich Bonhoeffer is not that he died at the hands of the Gestapo but that he reflected, prayed, wrote, counseled, and lived under the extreme circumstances of a Gestapo regime. His thoughts and ideas take on compelling significance simply because he worked them out under conditions where lesser persons would have been preoccupied with problems of personal survival. When Bonhoeffer wrote, in his *Letters and Papers from Prison,* about a future time of no religion at all or of a religionless Christianity, we can accept the seriousness of that description not because Bonhoeffer had read thoroughly the sociological literature on secularization but because he was on the extreme margin of society and in a position to see the vast disproportion between the real world of his time and the pretensions of church institutions.

The example of Dietrich Bonhoeffer sets forth the saintly personality in the most extreme of positions. Not all the saints have found themselves in such dramatic situations. Father Damien Deveuster (died 1889), a Belgian missionary in Hawaii, made himself a voluntary exile on the island of Molokai, where he ministered to a miserable leper colony for decades. His work much misunderstood (no less a personage than Robert Louis Stevenson came to his defense against those who libeled his name), Father Damien was cut off from the outside world because of his chosen work. Even when he went to confession, he stood in an open boat alongside a ship and shouted his sins up to a priest, who would lean over the ship's rail to hear him. He lived with the people of the island (all lepers, except himself) for decades. Eventually, he contracted the disease himself. Playwrights and novelists have made much of the manner he made his affliction public. At Sunday Mass, instead of the usual greeting of "Dear Brothers and Sisters" at the beginning of the sermon, he simply began "We lepers." His life was marked by a dramatic decision (to go to Molokai) and that decision—his second "conversion," if you will—was honed and perfected through a lifelong fidelity to the consequences of that decision done with equanimity and love. He died of his disease and its complication; he had given his life for his neighbors.

Saints, then, are for others because their perception of God's action in their lives drives them to others. In an interesting study of medieval hagiography, Alexander Murray has argued that the saints (who more often than not came from the "upper classes," despite the odd peasant or two) were "socially amphibious," that is, they transcended class—and medieval society was very class conscious—to find acceptance at all social levels.[3] The saint was one who could speak to all persons without respect to that person's status, just as the saint could minister to all despite the fact that his ministrations could be considered beneath his station. This ability to cross class lines was not merely a democratic impulse. It was a quite different way of relating to the world of people. It hinted at and gave credibility to the idea of the universality of the Christian message and paid tribute to the example of Saint Paul, who "became all things to all persons." This capacity for giving was once summed up by that loveliest of medieval saints, himself once a pampered upper-middle-class child. In his *Last Testament,* Saint Francis wrote of his conversion in the simplest of terms: "To me, Brother Francis, the Lord thus gave the grace to do penance: when I was a sinner, I thought it too bitter a thing to look at lepers, and the Lord led me to them and taught me to be merciful."

The very humility of the saint, which made him socially amphibious, also made him, paradoxically enough, into a fearless speaker of the truth. Murray points out that a constant theme in medieval hagiography was the saint's capacity for frank speech *(parrhesia).* The outspoken character of the saint allowed him or her to treat everyone as an equal; and on the basis of equality, the saint could both commend and reprove. Fiercely zealous medieval reformers like Saint Romuald (founder of the Camaldolese Hermits) and John Gualbert were famous for their scathing denunciations of unworthy prelates and rapacious nobility. Women, not usually privy to matters of high policy at the time, could advise and chide both popes and emperors, as the well-remembered deeds of Joan of Arc, Catherine of Siena, and Clare of Assisi attest. Only *parrhesia* can explain the audacity of a Saint Bernard of Clairvaux writing a newly elected pope to warn him of the possible loss of his soul as a result of assuming the papacy. This much admired capacity for free speech in the medieval period lies behind the saintly denunciations to be found in the *Paradiso* of Dante, whether it is Saint Francis lamenting the corruption of his friars or Saint Peter fulminating against the scandals of the papacy.

Frank speech has a prophetic edge to it. The prophetic character of the saint's life derives from the fearless denunciation of religious failings or perversities perceived from the vantage point of clear allegiance to the life of perfection. The saint can be prophetic, however, without emulating the zeal of a Bernard of Clairvaux or a Saint Joan of Arc. The very kind of life that a saint lives in relative silence can be a fearful reproach to others who come into contact with it. Hagiography is filled with stories of humble lay religious who energized the spiritual life of a convent or priority by the simple, but powerful, example of their dedicated lives. The paradigmatic force of the saint causes, in others, first a sense of self-criticism and then the occasion for change. Furthermore, as I have already noted, the saint can demonstrate ways of action when the culture is bewildered or paralyzed.

The greatest of the saints have been those who have risen above the exigencies of a particular moment to show a new way. Saint Benedict of Nursia was not merely the father of Western monasticism. He generated a religious style of life that could survive the implosion of civil and urban values in the period of Rome's collapse as a political force in the West. Saint Francis of Assisi demonstrated the values of poverty and rendered a judgment on the god of mammon precisely at the time when the Church was at its material high-water mark. It is no accident that Innocent III was on the chair of Peter when Francis first conceived his mission; the major representation of papal prestige was the one who approved the primitive rule (now lost) of the Little Poor Man. John Henry Newman, in both his life and his work, demonstrated to the nineteenth century that one could rescue the latent riches of the Catholic theological tradition. Newman exemplified a powerful spirituality without any of the treacly piety of a Frederick Faber or the theological desiccations of the Roman school. Suspect and harried in his own time, Newman was a figure whose prophetic life was only fully appreciated in the next century, when the stored resources of his life became a model and source for Catholic renewal in our time.

Every age must relearn and reappropriate the Gospel. Every age does that by fits and starts. Every age recognizes its failures and in response often precipitates not successes, but crises. Our age is no exception. There has been a stream of conventional wisdom from Vatican II to the present that points to failure, flabbiness of will, and sheer muddle in the Church. Other Christian bodies have not been immune to these same criticisms, despite some muscle flexing from the Evangelicals and Fundamentalists. Whatever the specifics of the current crisis—one can chart the specifics from lack of discipline to the utterances of *Humanae Vitae*—one thing is very clear: Administrative reforms will not bring solutions. If by fiat the Vatican assented to all the demands of every reform group of every persuasion (hardly a possibility because reform groups are headed by Archbishop Lefebvres as well as Hans Küngs), the fundamental issue would still remain: How is the Gospel to be lived and why should it be followed? Women priests are peripheral except that they can make the Gospel credible and urgent. Divorced and remarried Catholics are only fully in the Church if they are still convinced that the sacramental and liturgical life of the Church means something in their lives.

It is precisely at this juncture that the Saint (as opposed to the saints) becomes absolutely crucial. The Saint is one who in this or that extreme cultural circumstance says, by life and word, that there is a way in which the life of the Gospel can be lived.

The Saint at this point may look very extreme to the saints. History does not give much comfort to those who hope that the saints will emulate the Saints. G. K. Chesterton was surely right when he slyly suggested that the last Franciscan was Saint Francis of Assisi. But that is not to say that the witness of the Saint is such that the impact of her life stops with that single person. The Saint gives one a mark against which others may measure progress or assess failure. Not everyone is called to a ministry of poverty like that of the Catholic Workers or is courageous enough to be a Solzhenitsyn, but no sensitive religious person can ignore the value of their witness. A Christian must feel more uncomfortable, more unexamined, and less smug by the very presence of such persons in our midst. Their life simultaneously passes judgment on us and gives us a measure against which we can test ourselves.

The extremity of the Saint inevitably causes confusion and dissension. Her effort may seem not only extreme but also paradoxical or quixotic. It is a fact of history that those who have been the most influential in changing the Church at a particular moment are those who suffered most from the Church to effect the change. Saint Francis endures as a spiritual force while the Poor Men of Lyons are a historical footnote and the followers of Peter Waldo are marginal sectarians. Newman suffered in silence and influences the Church today while Ignaz Döllinger interests only the historian of theology or the antiquarian. We glibly speak of Saint John of the Cross or piously make the *Exercises* of Saint Ignatius Loyola without any memory that in their own day, they were imprisoned by ecclesiastical authorities. It is from these "extremists" that change, reform, and new ways of incarnating the Gospel derive. Garry Wills has made the point with pungency: "So Rome is always dying (partially) from head down while being (in part) resurrected from feet up. New forms of life have come from unexpected places—from Athanasius at local councils, Benedict in the monasteries, Albertus and Thomas in the universities, Francis of Assisi in the lanes and roads, Ignatius alone with a penitent making *The Spiritual Exercises,* Xavier and Ricci out at the rim of the world, Newman and Acton in pamphlets and journals."[4]

What I have suggested to this point is that the saint can provide prophetic impulses for the good of the Church. Such impulses are often dramatic and unsettling. But the Saint also has a more modest role. The Saint is a sign of hope for the ordinary Christian. Each age has its own difficulties with the practice of faith as it meets the counterchallenges of the nonreligious sphere. The problem of faith in our time is cast in the peculiar language of the age, but the intensity of the problem is probably no different from that of previous eras. We often maintain the conceit that it is our age (which we half proudly and half fearfully call "post-Christian" or "post-industrial") that is uniquely hostile to the Gospel. But is that the case? Does the Christian intellectual face deeper challenges to her credibility than those of the eighteenth century? Serious students of the subject would not think so. Is the moral fabric of Christianity weaker now than that of the generations after the Black Death in the fourteenth century? Hardly. What is significant for our understanding of the "problem of faith" or the "crisis of belief" is that it is uniquely *our* problem and *our* crisis. It must be solved in the context of all the issues that help create the problem or generate the crisis for a particular historical epoch.

It is in this setting that one can view the Saint as a sign of hope when the pressures against the credibility of the Gospel are at their peak. When Western Christianity as an institution seemed cravenly

incapable of dealing with Hitlerism in Germany, it was the individual
—the Dietrich Bonhoeffers, Maximilian Kolbes, and their confreres
—who made it possible to salvage the vision of Christianity in a
totalitarian setting. Less dramatically, the followers of Mother Teresa
keep alive the idea of hope in the seemingly hopeless desert of a
Calcutta. Her witness says that people can help, sacrifices can and
should be made. Saints in such settings provide a dual function for
the larger religious body: Their lives judge the mediocrity of most
lives while providing models to be emulated either "all the way" or
in proportion to the actual potentialities of a person's individual
circumstance.

In the final analysis, the Saint is a charismatic gift for the Church
and for the world. Saintliness is not granted to a person for individual
personal salvation but to aid others on that path. Saintliness is for the
good of the Church and for the good of the Gospel. That may be
—indeed, is—the final test of the worth of the saint. The earlier
understanding of the role of Saints (that behind the formal canonization process, for example) emphasized the Saint as a sure intercessor.
The entire canonization process was geared to demonstrate that we
can have a reasonable confidence in the saint's heavenly status. With
such confidence, we could pray that the Saint would intercede for us
before the throne of God. As the more traditional theologians insisted, a decree of canonization meant the Church considered the
canonized person an example of authentic sanctity *(vera sanctitas)*
who was in heaven *(caelestis beatitudo)* and whose cult was reliable
(dignitas cultus).

The intercessory role of Saints has been a part of the devotional
life of Christians from its earliest days. Indeed, as we have seen, the
near equation of Saint and miracle worker in the first millenium of
Christianity saw the Saint as not much more than an intercessor
before God and in the affairs (through miracles) of the faithful. It is
unlikely that the intercessory elements of Christian piety will go
away; they are too deeply rooted in the common religious experience
of humanity. Indeed, there is no reason why such piety should disap-
pear. It is a universal impulse and is not phenomenologically dissimilar to the very human act of crying out to long-dead mothers or other

loved ones in time of crisis for succor and aid. The entire apparatus of the veneration of the saints at their shrines or through their relics has its civic and social counterparts, as any visitor to the shrine of the Unknown Soldier or participant in an Elvis Presley memorabilia auction can readily attest.

The function of intercession and the practice of veneration do not sum up, however, the meaning of the Saint. That is the point being urged here. I wish to focus on the saint not as object or icon but as flesh and blood personality. My concern has been with shifting attention from the hieratic figure of a Saint Christopher to the faith realities of a Saint Augustine of Hippo. What should concern us is the side of the saint that emphasizes the prophetic, the exemplary, the moral dimension, and the challenge. It is in that side of sanctity where we discover the rich potentialities of the Gospel enfleshed for our admiration and, more, emulation.

NOTES

1. Dag Hammarskjöld, *Markings* (New York: Knopf, 1964), p. 109.
2. Walker Percy, *The Moviegoer* (New York: Noonday Press, 1967), p. 13.
3. Alexander Murray, *Reason and Society in the Middle Ages* (Oxford: Clarendon Press, 1978), pp. 383–404.
4. Garry Wills, *Bare Ruined Choirs: Doubt, Prophecy, and Radical Religion* (Garden City: Doubleday, 1972), pp. 262–263.

Selected Bibliography

Abbott, Walter, et al, eds. *The Documents of Vatican II.* New York: Guild, 1966.

Amore, Agostino. "Culto e canonizzazione dei santi nell' antichitá cristiana." *Antonianum,* January–March 1977, pp. 38–80.

————. "La canonizzazione vescovile." *Antonianum,* April–September 1977, pp. 231–266.

Bernanos, George. *The Diary of a Country Priest.* New York: Macmillan, 1948.

Biblioteca Sanctorum, 12 vols. Rome: Istituto Giovanni XXIII, 1961.

Blehl, Vincent F., ed. *The Essential Newman.* New York: Mentor, 1963.

Bonhoeffer, D. *Letters and Papers From Prison.* New York: Macmillian, 1967.

The Book of Saints. New York: Crowell, 1921.

Bree, Germaine. *Albert Camus.* New York: Harcourt Brace Jovanovich, 1961.

Brown, Peter. *Saint Augustine of Hippo.* London: Faber, 1967.

Bruteau, Beatrice. "Neo-Feminism and the New Revolution in Consciousness." *Cross Currents,* Summer 1977, pp. 170–181.

Butler, Alban, et al. *Lives of the Saints,* 4 vols. New York: Kenedy, 1956.

Camus, Albert. *The Plague.* New York: Vintage, 1963.

Carretto, Carlo. *Letters From the Desert.* Maryknoll: Orbis, 1972.

Carrouges, Michael. *Soldier of the Spirit: The Life of Charles De Foucauld.* New York: Putnam, 1956.

Clarke, John, ed. *Saint Thérèse of Lisieux: The Story of A Soul.* Washington: Institute of Carmelite Studies, 1975.

————. *Saint Thérèse of Lisieux: Last Conversations.* Washington: Institute of Carmelite Studies, 1977.

Codex Juris Canonici. Vatican City: Typis Polyglottis Vaticanis, 1956.

Cox, Harvey. *The Feast of Fools.* Cambridge: Harvard University Press, 1969.

Cunningham, Lawrence. *Brother Francis.* New York: Harper and Row, 1972.

_____. *Saint Francis of Assisi.* Boston: Twayne, 1976.

_____. "The Anti-Exodus of Elie Wiesel." In *Responses to Elie Wiesel,* edited by Harry Cargas. New York: Persea Books, 1977.

Daly, Mary. *Gyn/Ecology: A Metaethics of Radical Feminism.* Boston: Beacon, 1979.

DeFerrari, Roy, ed. *Early Christian Biographies.* Washington: Fathers of the Church, 1952.

Delehaye, Hippolyte. *The Legends of the Saints.* New York: Fordham, 1962.

DeLubac, Henri. *Teilhard de Chardin: The Man and His Meaning.* New York: Mentor, 1964.

Dolan, John, ed. *The Essential Erasmus.* New York: Mentor, 1964.

Dunne, John. *The Reasons of the Heart.* Notre Dame: University of Notre Dame, 1978.

Etzioni, Amitai. *A Comprehensive Analysis of Complex Organizations.* New York: Free Press, 1961.

Finley, M. I., ed. *Studies in Ancient Society.* London: Routledge and Kegan Paul, 1974.

Farmer, D. H., ed. *The Oxford Dictionary of Saints.* Oxford: Clarendon, 1978.

Frankfort, Henri, et al. *Before Philosophy: The Intellectual Adventure of Ancient Man.* Baltimore: Penguin, 1961.

Fremantle, Anne. *Desert Calling.* London: Hollis and Carter, 1950.

Frend, H. C. *Martyrdom and Persecution in the Early Church.* Garden City: Doubleday Anchor, 1967.

Geary, Patrick. *Furta Sacra: The Theft of Relics in the Middle Ages.* Princeton: Princeton University Press, 1978.

Graef, Hilda. *Mystics of Our Times.* Paramus: Paulist, 1963.

Green, Thomas. "The Revision of Canon Law." *Theological Studies,* December 1979, pp. 593–679.

Greene, Graham. *The Lawless Roads.* London: Heineman, 1939.

_____. *The Power and the Glory.* New York: Viking, 1940.

_____. *The Human Factor.* New York: Simon and Schuster, 1978.

Guarducci, Margerita. *La tomba di San Pietro.* Rome: Studium, 1959.

Habig, Marion, ed. *Saint Francis of Assisi: Omnibus of Sources.* Chicago: Franciscan Herald Press, 1973.

Hammarskjöld, Dag. *Markings.* New York: Knopf, 1964.

Hart, Patrick, ed. *Thomas Merton: The Monastic Journey.* Garden City: Doubleday Image, 1978.

Heer, M. *The Medieval World.* New York: Mentor, 1978.

Hertling, L., et al. *The Roman Catacombs.* Milwaukee: Bruce, 1960.

Huizinga, J. *The Waning of the Middle Ages.* Garden City: Doubleday Anchor, 1954.

Hurley, Neil. *A Theology of Film.* New York: Harper and Row, 1970.

————. *The Reel Revolution.* Maryknoll: Orbis, 1978.

James, William. *The Varieties of Religious Experience.* New York: Mentor, 1958.

Johnston, William. *The Inner Eye of Love.* New York: Harper and Row, 1978.

Jones, Chesyln, ed. *The Study of the Liturgy.* New York: Oxford University Press, 1978.

Jungmann, J. *The Early Liturgy.* Notre Dame: University of Notre Dame Press, 1959.

Kelly, J. N. D. *Saint Jerome.* New York: Harper and Row, 1977.

Kirch, Conradus, ed. *Enchiridion Fontium Historiae Ecclesiasticae Antiquae.* Rome: Herder, 1960.

Knowles, David. *Great Historical Enterprises.* New York: Nelson, 1962.

Küng, Hans. *On Being a Christian.* Garden City: Doubleday, 1976.

Kunkel, Francis. *The Labyrinthine Ways of Graham Greene.* New York: Sheed and Ward, 1959.

Latourelle, René. "La Sainteté signe de la Révelátion." *Gregorianum XLVI* (1965), pp. 36–65.

Lewis, R. W. B. *The Picaresque Saint.* Philadelphia: Lippincott, 1958.

Lunn, Arnold. *A Saint in the Slave Trade.* New York: Sheed and Ward, 1947.

McClendon, James W. *Biography as Theology.* Nashville: Abingdon, 1974.

McGinley, Phyllis. *Saint Watching.* Garden City: Doubleday Image, 1974.

Marrucchi, Orazio. *Christian Epigraphy.* Chicago: Ares, 1964.

Merton, Thomas. *Disputed Questions.* New York: Farrar, Straus, and Giroux, 1960.

————. *The Wisdom of the Desert.* New York: New Directions, 1970.

————. *Contemplative Prayer.* Garden City: Doubleday Image, 1971.

————. *Contemplation in a World of Action.* Garden City: Doubleday Image, 1973.

————. *Asian Journal.* New York: New Directions, 1973.

Mooney, Christopher. *Teilhard de Chardin and the Mystery of Christ.* Garden City: Doubleday Image, 1969.

Murray, Alexander. *Religion and Society in the Middle Ages.* Oxford: Clarendon, 1978.

Neville, Robert. *Soldier, Sage, Saint.* New York: Fordham University Press, 1978.

New Catholic Encyclopedia, 15 vols. New York: McGraw Hill, 1967.

Nicolau, M., et al. *Sacrae Theologiae Summa.* 4 vols. Madrid: BAC, 1955.

Percy, Walker. *The Moviegoer.* New York: Noonday, 1967.
_____. *Love in the Ruins.* New York: Dell, 1972.
_____. *The Message in the Bottle.* New York: Farrar, Straus, and Giroux, 1975.
Quasten, Johannes. *Patrology,* 3 vols. Westminster: Newman, 1950.
Rahner, Karl. "The Church of the Saints." In *Theological Investigations,* vol. 3. Baltimore: Helicon, 1967.
_____. *Foundations of Christian Faith.* New York: Seabury, 1977.
Rahner, Karl, et al., eds. *Sacramentum Mundi,* 6 vols. New York: Herder and Herder, 1969.
Rubenstein, Richard. *The Cunning of History.* New York: Harper and Row, 1975.
Schimmel, A. M. *The Mystical Element in Islam.* Chapel Hill: University of North Carolina Press, 1977.
Schmidt, Hermann. *Introductio in Liturgiam Occidentialem.* Rome: Herder, 1960.
Schneidau, Herbert. *Sacred Discontent: The Bible in the Western Tradition.* Berkeley: University of California Press, 1976.
Silone, Ignazio. *Bread and Wine.* New York: Signet Classic, 1962.
_____. *The Spiritual Exercises of Saint Ignatius Loyola.* Garden City: Doubleday Image, 1964.
Teilhard de Chardin, Pierre. *Letters From a Traveller.* New York: Harper and Row, 1962.
_____. *The Heart of Matter.* New York: Harcourt Brace Jovanovich, 1979.
TeSelle, Sallie. *Speaking in Parables.* Philadelphia: Fortress, 1975.
Tillich, Paul. *Systematic Theology,* 3 vols. in one. Chicago: University of Chicago Press, 1967.
Traversi, Derek. *T. S. Eliot: The Longer Poems.* New York: Harcourt Brace Jovanovich, 1976.
Trouncer, Margaret. *Charles de Foucauld.* London: Harrop, 1972.
Van der Leeuw, G. *Religion in Essence and Manifestation,* 2 vols. New York: Harper Torchbooks, 1960.
Ware, Timothy. *The Orthodox Church.* Baltimore: Penguin, 1963.
Wildier, N. M. *Teilhard de Chardin: An Introduction.* New York: Harper and Row, 1968.
Wills, Garry. *Bare Ruined Choirs: Doubt, Prophecy and Radical Religion.* Garden City: Doubleday, 1972.
Yates, Gayle. *What We Want: The Ideas of a Movement.* Cambridge: Harvard University Press, 1975.
Zahn, Gordon. *In Solitary Witness: The Life and Death of Franz Jägerstatter.* Boston: Beacon, 1968.
Ziolkowski, Theodore. *Fictional Transfigurations of Jesus.* Princeton: Princeton University Press, 1972.

Index